CONTROVERSIAL ESSAYS

CONTROVERSIAL ESSAYS

Thomas Sowell

HOOVER INSTITUTION PRESS
Stanford University   Stanford, California

www.hoover.org

Hoover Institution Press Publication No. 511

Hoover Institution at the Leland Stanford Junior University,
Stanford, California 94305-6003

First printing 2002
24 23 22 21   13 12 11 10 9

Manufactured in the United States of America

The paper used in this publication meets the minimum requirements of the American National Standard for Information Sciences— Permanence of Paper for Printed Library Materials, ANSI/NISO Z39.48–1992. ∞

Library of Congress Cataloging-in-Publication Data

Sowell, Thomas, 1930–

Controversial essays / Thomas Sowell.

pages cm — (Hoover institution press publication ; no. 511)

ISBN-13: 978-0-8179-2992-3 (pbk : alk. paper)

ISBN-13: 978-0-8179-2993-0 (ePub)

ISBN-13: 978-0-8179-2997-8 (mobi)

ISBN-13: 978-0-8179-2998-5 (PDF)

1. African Americans—Social conditions—1975– . 2. Minorities—United States—Social conditions. 3. United States—Politics and government—1989– . 4. United States—Race relations. 5. United States—Social conditions—1980– . I. Title. II. Series: Hoover Institution Press publication ; 511.

E839.5.S63 2002

973.92   2002027327

CONTENTS

PART III: POLITICAL ISSUES

PART IV: EDUCATIONAL ISSUES

PART VII: RANDOM THOUGHTS

PREFACE

These essays first appeared in my nationally syndicated newspaper column, and the favorable responses they received from readers have led to their being reprinted here. Many of the events which provoked these writings raised questions that went beyond the passing episodes involved. This was especially so where economic issues were involved, for these same fundamental issues recur in the economy over the years—and centuries—in various guises. Similarly, racial issues in the United States today involve many of the same principles that have been controversial in relations between various racial and ethnic groups in other countries and in other times.

In addition to the very serious issues raised in many of these essays, there are also some lighter subjects and even the serious issues sometimes have their lighter aspects. Without a sense of humor, politics would be too painful to bear.

Special thanks must go to the Hoover Institution and to Stanford University, whose rich research sources made informed commentary on a wide variety of subjects possible, and to my assistant Na Liu, whose diligent work unearthed the information that I needed. Finally, acknowledgement is also due to Karen Duryea of Creators Syndicate, who caught errors in spelling, grammar, syntax, and facts that might otherwise have slipped in these columns, to my chagrin. The same thanks must go to a conscientious copy-editor at the Hoover Institution Press who caught some more lapses of mine.

Thomas Sowell

PART I
ECONOMIC ISSUES

DRUGS AND POLITICS

A tourist in New York's Greenwich Village had his portrait sketched by a sidewalk artist, who charged him $100.

"That's expensive," the tourist said. "But it's a great sketch, so I'll pay it. But, really, it took you only five minutes."

"Twenty years and five minutes," the artist replied.

The same misconception of costs runs through the much more serious issue of the prices of medicine and government regulation of those prices. When a pill whose ingredients cost a quarter is sold for two dollars, that is an open invitation to demagogues to begin loudly denouncing the pharmaceutical drug company's "obscene" and "unconscionable" profits at the expense of the sick. But the people who are doing this are counting only the five minutes and ignoring the twenty years.

The physical ingredients of the medicine are its cheapest ingredients. The ingredient that costs millions of dollars—sometimes hundreds of millions—is the knowledge gained from years of research, and trial and error, which finally results in the creation of a new medicine. That is what the price of the pills has to cover, if we expect investors to continue to pour vast sums of money into drug companies that are trying to discover new cures for such diseases as cancer, AIDS and Alzheimer's.

Other companies, manufacturing generic equivalents, pay

only the costs of the physical ingredients, having copied the enormously expensive formula free of charge—legitimately after the patent has expired and not so legitimately in other countries, where patent laws are not taken as seriously as in the United States. The company that simply uses someone else's formula free of charge can sell the same pill for 35 cents and still make a profit.

Somebody has to pay the high costs of discovery or the development of new drugs will be slower and therefore more people will needlessly suffer and die. While allowing patent laws to be over-ridden by politicians allows some people to buy the drug at low prices, based on the low current costs of manufacturing the medicine, that just leaves the far greater overhead costs of creating these medicines to be paid by others.

Worst of all, it leaves the even higher costs of needless pain, suffering and premature death to be paid by those whose relief is delayed for years by policies like these, which slow down the development of new medicines to cure their afflictions.

The United States has been one of the few countries resisting political pressures to impose price controls on pharmaceutical drugs, or to water down the patent laws which allow the original discoverer of new drugs to have a monopoly for a fixed number of years, so as to recover the costs of discovery before other companies get to use their formula free of charge.

The United States also produces a wholly disproportionate share of all the new life-saving drugs in the world. But politicians ignore this connection. Other countries have scientists capable of developing new medicines, but the economics and politics of the situation discourage companies in those countries from making the huge investments made by American pharmaceutical companies under American patent law.

Unfortunately, the Bush administration has recently begun to cave in to the demagogues at home and abroad. After Congressional liberals like Ted Kennedy, Henry Waxman, and Charles Schumer began making noises about a need to get the drug Cipro cheaper because of the anthrax scare, the administration threatened to over-ride the patent for the drug unless the manufacturer supplied it at a cheaper rate.

The retail price of Cipro was $5 a pill and the government itself says that someone stricken with anthrax needs to take two pills a day for five days and cheaper antibiotics thereafter. Is $50 too much to pay to save your life? And is it worth jeopardizing a whole system that has made this country the leading creator of life-saving drugs, just to get the demagogues off the Bush administration's back politically?

The administration also caved at a recent international conference in Qatar, where foreign countries gained the right to set aside international patent agreements whenever they choose to decree a public health "emergency." This allows them a free ride on costly American research, at least until they kill the goose that lays the golden egg—new life-saving medicines in this case.

THE
REAL
REVOLUTIONARIES

The twentieth century was, among other things, a century of revolutions—not only bloody uprisings and military coups, but also revolutions in science, politics and in the way people live. However, as much as the political left loves to use words like "change" and "revolution" as if they had a monopoly or a copyright on them, the actual track record of the left pales in comparison with the social revolutions created by the free market.

No government of the left has done as much for the poor as capitalism has. Even when it comes to the redistribution of income, the left talks the talk but the free market walks the walk.

What do the poor most need? They need to stop being poor. And how can that be done, on a mass scale, except by an economy that creates vastly more wealth? Yet the political left has long had a remarkable lack of interest in how wealth is created. As far as they are concerned, wealth exists *somehow* and the only interesting question is how to redistribute it.

The history of the American economy in the twentieth century was an incredible story of the luxuries of the rich becoming commonplace among the masses and even the poor. When liberal and radical intellectuals speak of a period of "change," they almost never mention the 1920s, because it was not an era of the kinds of political changes they favor. But it was a pivotal decade of change in the material well-being and expansion of the horizons of most Americans, including the poor.

It was during the 1920s that electricity, the automobile and radio reached the masses, when motion pictures came of age and began to talk. While technology and mass production spearheaded the changes of the 1920s, this was also a decade that saw a revolution in more efficient distribution systems through grocery and department store chains that brought the cost of many goods and services down within the reach of ordinary Americans.

All this added up to a social revolution—but it was not "change" as defined by the intelligentsia, because it happened independently of them and of the government, and was not part of any master plan or ideological crusade.

As late as 1930, most American homes did not have a refrigerator but, by the end of the decade, most did. By 1970, virtually all families living in poverty had refrigerators. By 1994, most American households below the poverty line had a microwave oven and a videocassette recorder—things that less than one percent of all American households had in 1971.

All of this went into raising the standard of living of the average American. It was not political rhetoric, mass rallies or poses of moral indignation that gave the people a better life. It was capitalism.

Even in the homeland of socialism, the Soviet Union, it was capitalists who created much of the industrialization for which the Communists took credit. The first new automobile factory built under the Communists was built by the Ford Motor Company. Germany's Krupp and I. G. Farben were also key builders of Soviet industry, along with DuPont, RCA, International Harvester and others from the capitalist world.

Even when it comes to the redistribution of wealth that is at the heart of the ideology of the left, the market does it better. Most American millionaires did not inherit their wealth, but created it themselves. As for the poor, imagine anyone so radical as to promise to move the bottom 20 percent of Americans out of that bracket within a decade and put more of them up in the top 20 percent than were left back where they were originally.

Yet this happens regularly and with no fanfare in the American economy. But even a big change in the distribution of income like this does not count with those who talk about income brackets and ignore the actual flesh-and-blood people who move in and out of those brackets. Most people who were in the bottom 20 percent in 1975 were in the top 20 percent at some point before 1992.

The poor will always be with us, so long as they are defined as the bottom 20 percent, even if yesterday's bottom 20 percent are now among "the rich," as such terms are defined by those with a stereotyped vision of a static world.

Dynamic income changes among people are concealed by talking about brackets, as if the same people stayed in those brackets. The left cannot accept the kind of income redistribution that does not fit their vision. These and other benefits of a free market will certainly never be called a "public service."

INDIA
UNBOUND

There are few things more heartwarming than watching people rise out of poverty to a better life. When it is a whole nation in the process of doing so, it is especially inspiring. That is the theme of a marvelous new book titled *India Unbound* by Indian hi-tech entrepreneur Gurcharan Das.

In a well-blended combination of facts, history and personal experiences, the author spells out how and why India took so long after achieving independence from Britain in 1947 before its economy began to improve dramatically after the 1991 reforms that allowed more of a free market to operate. That was a decisive turning point, with businesses no longer being suffocated by some of the most pervasive and intrusive government controls in the world.

Before the reforms, Indian entrepreneurs could not make the most basic decisions about their own businesses without permission from an army of government bureaucrats. Decisions about hiring, firing (virtually impossible), expanding output or ordering raw material were all subject to the whims, the delays and the extortions of bribes by petty officials who knew little and cared less about the realities of business.

The Indian entrepreneur "has to bribe from twenty to forty functionaries if he is serious about doing business." Moreover, he must "grovel" before these petty tyrants who have been armed with the power to say "yea" or "nay" to a sweeping range of business plans. Even some of India's biggest and most distinguished enterprises, the Tata industries, had more than a hundred proposals to start new businesses or expand old ones end up "in the wastebaskets of the bureaucrats."

Another great Indian industrial empire, that of the Birla family, was likewise refused the government permissions needed to expand. The net result was that they bought pulp in Canada, had it converted to fiber in Thailand, had the fiber converted to yarn in Indonesia and then had the yarn made into carpets in Belgium. All the while, India remained a very poor country in need of economic growth and the jobs and incomes that these operations could have provided.

At one time, it was a violation of the law to produce more output than you were authorized to produce by the government. A manufacturer of cold medicines was fearful that his sales had overshot the mark during a flu epidemic and had to have a lawyer spend months preparing a legal defense, in case he was hauled before a government commission.

Gurcharan Das is careful to point out that these and many other economically disastrous policies grew out of good intentions. Indian leaders from Jawaharlal Nehru to his daughter Indira Gandhi put their faith in the government-planned economy and distrusted both businesses and the consuming public. What they lacked in any serious knowledge of business or markets they made up in socialist dogma and smug self-righteousness.

When the head of the Tata industries tried to explain some facts of life to Nehru, the prime minister's response was: "Never talk to me about profit, Jeh, it is a dirty word."

Though the Indian statist leaders thought of themselves as looking out for the poor, their policies have been estimated to have held back economic development to the point where the average Indian's income would have been hundreds of dollars a year greater without their restrictions. In a country with millions of very poor people, some suffering from malnutrition, the loss of a few hundred dollars in annual income meant far more than it would have meant to the average American.

Like so many socialistic policies around the world, those in India were not relaxed or ended because of better understanding but because of bitter experience. When these policies had the Indian government on the verge of bankruptcy, its leaders had no choice but to make fundamental changes in the economy, in order to qualify for help from the International Monetary Fund and the World Bank.

After the 1991 reforms freed Indian entrepreneurs from suffocating government controls, the economy took off. Growth rates reached new heights, Indian businesses expanded and foreign investments poured in. The kind of hi-tech success that Indians had achieved in Silicon Valley they now began to achieve in India.

Although this is a book about India, many of its lessons are universal—and have not yet been learned by American political, intellectual and media elites.

CAPITAL GAINS
AND
"TRICKLE DOWN"

Among the suggestions being made for getting the American economy moving up again is a reduction in the capital gains tax. But any such suggestion makes people on the left go ballistic. It is "trickle-down" economics, they cry.

Liberals claim that those who favor tax cuts and a free market want to help the rich first, hoping that the benefits they receive will eventually trickle down to the masses of ordinary people. But there has never been any school of economists who believed in a trickle-down theory. No such theory can be found in even the most voluminous and learned books on the history of economics. It is a straw man.

This straw man is not confined to the United States. A critic of India's change from a government-dominated economy to more free market activity in the 1990s accused those behind this change of having "blind faith in the 'trickle-down' theory of distributing the benefits of economic growth among different socio-economic groups in the country." But free-market economics is not about "distributing" anything to anybody. It is about letting people earn whatever they can from voluntary transactions with other people.

Those who imagine that profits first benefit business owners—and that benefits only belatedly trickle down to workers—have the sequence completely backwards. When an investment is made, whether to build a railroad or to open a new restaurant, the first money is spent hiring people to do the work. Without that, nothing happens. Money goes out first to pay expenses and then comes back as profits later—if at all. The high rate of failure of new businesses makes painfully clear that there is nothing inevitable about the money coming back.

Even with successful businesses, years can elapse between the initial investment and the return of earnings. From the time when an oil company begins spending money to explore for petroleum to the time when the first gasoline resulting from that exploration comes out of a pump at a filling station, a decade may have passed. In the meantime, all sorts of employees have been paid—geologists, engineers, refinery workers, truck drivers.

Nor is the oil industry unique. No one who begins publishing a newspaper expects to break even—much less make a profit—during the first year or two. But reporters and other members of the newspaper staff expect to be paid every payday, even while the paper shows only red ink on the bottom line.

In short, the sequence of payments is directly the opposite of what is assumed by those who talk about a "trickle-down" theory. As for capital gains, some countries don't tax capital gains at all. They tax a business' earnings, but not capital gains, which are harder to define and sometimes illusory.

The real effect of a reduction in the capital gains tax rate is that it opens the prospect—only the prospect—of greater future net profits. But that is enough to provide incentives for making current investments. Reductions in the capital gains tax rate tend to draw money out of tax shelters like municipal bonds and into creating jobs and productive capacity. That's the point!

As with all taxes, a distinction must be made between tax rates and tax revenues. Tax revenues went up while tax rates went down in the 1980s. Similarly in the 1960s and the 1920s. That is because incomes rose more than tax rates fell. But still it will be claimed that we cannot "afford" to cut tax rates because it would create deficits. Spending creates deficits—and it is big spenders who fight hardest against cutting tax rates.

It is not faith but empirical evidence that is overwhelming on the actual track record of tax cuts and free markets. By the 1980s, this mounting evidence convinced even left-wing governments in various parts of the world to cut back government operations and sell government-owned enterprises to private industry. Faith had nothing to do with it.

In India, in the decade since the 1991 economic reforms which were condemned as "blind faith," the country's economic growth rate has soared. It has been estimated that the real blind faith—in government planning—had cost the average Indian hundreds of dollars a year in income during the decades when socialist dogma ruled. In a poor country like India, this was income they could not afford to miss. Even in a prosperous country like the United States, there is no need to forego economic benefits for the sake of a political phrase.

NO SENSE
OF
PROPORTION

Mathematicians use the term "rational numbers" for numbers that can form a ratio. By this definition, there is a lot of irrationality in California, where many people seem incapable of forming a ratio or proportion between different things.

California's electricity crisis is a result of years of refusing to have any sense of proportion between the desirability of environmental goals and the desirability of having electricity. Yet apparently the state's politicians have learned nothing from any of this.

Having provoked an electricity crisis and a financial crisis by imposing impossible conditions on public utilities, the California government is now imposing similarly irrational conditions on the automobile industry by requiring them to produce a certain quota of electric cars for sale in the state, as a precondition to their selling any other cars in California.

The purpose of the electric cars is to reduce the air pollution created by cars that burn gasoline. Obviously, no one is in favor of polluted air, but the question is whether the desirable goal of reducing pollution is to be pursued in utter disregard of other desirable things.

Electric cars may be fun at amusement parks, where they don't have to go very far or very fast. But if the consuming public wanted electric cars for regular use, Detroit would be manufacturing them by the millions. Only people infatuated with their own wonderful specialness would think that their job is to coerce both the manufacturers and the consuming public into something that neither of them wants.

California seems to have more than its fair share of self-infatuated people proclaiming utopian notions. Worse yet, such people are indulged by the media, the political system and the courts, while the enormous costs they create are quietly loaded onto unsuspecting consumers and taxpayers.

Somebody is going to have to pay for these electric cars that the public does not want. State agencies can buy some of them with the taxpayers' money. Some private individuals and organizations may be subjected to pressure from the state government to buy them. And some electric cars may just sit on dealers' lots or in storage, gathering dust. But they are still all going to have to be paid for by somebody because there is no free lunch.

Maybe those who imposed these new requirements think that the automobile companies can be forced to absorb the losses. Imposing costs on people out of state is a ploy that has been tried before with electricity. But apparently some people never learn.

Nothing is easier than glib enthusiasm for the benefits of electric cars—and some of those benefits may even be real. But there is still the need to have a sense of proportion, because there are other benefits that will have to be sacrificed and other costs that will have to be paid.

Electric automobile engines are not powerful enough to move full-size cars at any reasonable speed, so that means people have to drive around in flimsy vehicles that can easily become death traps in an accident. Make no mistake about it, air pollution increases the incidence of fatal diseases. But will more people die from that than from traffic deaths in flimsy

cars? People who are crusading for electric cars are not interested in that ratio.

Cars running on electricity may create no air pollution
themselves, but the electricity has to come from somewhere
to charge and re-charge the batteries that run these cars. What
difference does it make if the car itself creates no pollution but
the pollution occurs at an electric power plant, miles away,
that is the ultimate source of the energy that moves the car?

Why doesn't the public want to buy electric cars? Because
in real life you have to be able to get where you want to go, in
some reasonable time, whether or not your destination is
within the narrow range of an electric car's batteries. And you
want to be able to turn around and come back when you are
ready, not have to wait for hours to re-charge your batteries
for the return trip.

You may not get there at all if you are oozing down a highway in a fragile little vehicle that is out of sync with the fast-
moving heavy traffic around you. But none of this matters to
people who are not in the habit of weighing one thing against
another. Nor do such people want to allow other people to
weigh one thing against another for themselves, rather than
have their choices dictated from on high. No sense of proportion.

HEADLINE
NEWS

The obvious continues to make headlines in California. "Federal price limits backfire" read the big front-page headline in the *San Francisco Chronicle*. These price limits are the federally imposed "caps" on electricity prices that California Governor Gray Davis has been clamoring for, backed up by Congressional Democrats.

"Some generators withhold power rather than abide by rate caps" the news story said. Where there are high costs of generating or transmitting electricity, the price caps in western states can make selling electricity to these states unprofitable or even create losses for the electricity suppliers.

Although officials in both California and Nevada had urged the Federal Energy Regulatory Commission to impose price controls on electricity, they now concluded that "the newly imposed limits have had the unintended consequence of increasing a threat of blackouts in the two states." In other words, people supply less when you reduce the price they will be paid. This news is literally thousands of years old.

People withheld supplies when price controls were imposed in the days of the Roman Empire. George Washington's troops nearly starved at Valley Forge when price controls were imposed on food. During the French revolution, there were likewise price controls on food, with the result that "as soon as we fixed the price of wheat and rye we saw no more of those grains."

When President Nixon imposed controls on meat prices in 1973, much American cattle began to be exported, mostly to Canada, rather than being supplied to the U.S. market. Price controls on gasoline had motorists waiting in long lines at filling stations, sometimes for hours. But there have been no such gas lines for the past 20 years, since Ronald Reagan got rid of these price controls as one of his first acts after becoming president in 1981.

Price controls have had the same effect around the world, for centuries on end, among people of every race, color and creed, and under governments ranging from the most democratic to the most totalitarian. Why then is everyone so surprised that price controls on electricity in the western states seem to be reducing the supply of electricity there, creating rolling blackouts in Nevada and threatening more of the same in California?

Part of the reason—aside from widespread ignorance of both economics and history—is that a very successful political propaganda campaign has depicted opposition to price controls as being based on nothing but "ideology" or "theory." These words were repeated endlessly in the media by Democrats in California and Washington, as they sought to pressure the Federal Energy Regulatory Commission to impose price controls, or at least embarrass President Bush for opposing such controls.

Far from being a theory or an ideology, the effects of price controls on supply have been confirmed by facts as consistently as anything outside the realm of pure science. What the attempt to reduce this to mere ideology is saying is that there couldn't possibly be any real reason to be against price controls, unless you were just a lackey for the power companies.

This whole political game has been played before—and with disastrous effects for the public. One of the reasons price controls on oil were not repealed when other price controls were ended back in the 1970s was that a political propaganda campaign had demonized oil companies as the cause of the shortage of gasoline.

All sorts of charges and rumors were spread about the nefarious machinations of oil companies as the cause of all our troubles. Extensive government and private investigations failed to substantiate any of these charges and rumors. Nevertheless, the smear stuck and no politician wanted to be seen as caving in to Big Oil by ending price controls on petroleum.

In other words, a wholly needless problem of shortages was created and sustained by the demonizing of those who produced the product that was needed. That is exactly what is now happening with electricity.

Scarcely a day goes by without California Governor Gray Davis making sweeping accusations against electricity suppliers—"robber barons" he calls them—and the polls show that these accusations are working. California's attorney general is threatening lawsuits and criminal indictments against power companies. All this is great political theater but none of this will keep the lights on or the machinery of industry running.

WARRIOR IN
A 200-YEAR
WAR

The death of Julian Simon was a special loss because he was one of those people who took on the thankless task of talking sense on a subject where nonsense is all the rage. A professor of economics at the University of Maryland, Julian Simon wrote fact-filled books about population—all of them exposing the fallacies of those who were promoting "overpopulation" hysteria.

Ironically, Professor Simon's death occurred during the 200th anniversary of Malthus' *Essay on the Principle of Population* which started the hysteria that is still with us today, despite two centuries of mounting evidence against it. Like so many other theories that can survive tons of contrary evidence, overpopulation theory relies on slippery definitions and a constituency that needs a mission more than it wants facts.

What Malthus said two centuries ago was that human beings have the potential to increase faster than the food needed to feed them. No one doubted this—then or now. From this he made the fatal leap across a chasm of logic to say that there was a real danger that people would in fact grow so fast as to create a problem of feeding them.

The truism that the capacity to produce food limits the size of the sustainable population does not mean that population is anywhere near those limits. No automobile can drive faster than the power of its engine will permit, but you cannot explain the actual speeds of cars on roads and highways by those limits, because only an idiot drives at those limits.

Julian Simon set out to explain what happened to real population in the real world, not what happens in abstract models or popular hysteria. In the real world, as he demonstrated with masses of facts and in-depth analysis, we are nowhere near to running low on food or natural resources.

Professor Simon made a famous bet with the leading hysteria-monger of our time, Paul Ehrlich of Stanford University. Simon had offered to bet anybody that any set of natural resources that they claimed were running low would in fact be cheaper in the future than today. Professor Ehrlich took him up on it. Simon allowed Ehrlich to pick which resources and which period of time.

Ehrlich and his fellow hysterics chose a bundle of ten natural resources and a period of ten years. At the end of the decade, not only was the real cost of that bundle lower than at the beginning, every single natural resource that the Ehrlich camp had picked had a lower real cost than when the decade began.

If we were really running low on these resources, they would be getting progressively more expensive, instead of progressively cheaper. This is elementary supply-and-demand economics. But those addicted to overpopulation hysteria are no more interested in economics than they are in evidence.

What overpopulation theory provides is far more emotionally satisfying than facts, logic or economics. It is one of a whole family of theories which depict other people as so dangerously thoughtless that imposing the superior wisdom and virtue of some anointed social missionaries is all that can save us from disaster.

This vision inspired the eugenics movement in the early decades of this century, the recycling movement today and innumerable other heady crusades in between. Contrary facts mean absolutely nothing to the true believers. Those who insist on talking about those contrary facts encounter only hostility and demonization.

Julian Simon understood that. In a letter to me a couple of years ago, he mentioned a certain Nobel Prize-winning economist who had said to him that "even with all his prestige he would not say that population growth might well be a good thing because he was afraid he might lose credibility." Such is the power of intimidation in our time.

"Yes, one can always argue that such prudence is wise. But we all know the consequences of such 'wise' choices," Simon wrote. It is a society where strident hysteria drowns out truth and where our policies are based on headstrong nonsense, loudly shouted.

With a full understanding of the opposition and smears he would encounter, Julian Simon nevertheless wrote *The Economics of Population Growth, Population Matters* and—his best-known book—*The Ultimate Resource*. To him, the ultimate resource was human intelligence.

We should also add, in honor of Julian Simon, the courage to use that intelligence.

THE ROLE
OF
THE RICH

A recent catalogue from the giant second-hand camera dealer KEH listed a Canon camera made for the Japanese navy during World War II. This model is described as one of only 15 such cameras made and as being still in excellent condition. Its price is $40,000.

Most of us who shop for second-hand camera equipment aren't planning to pay 40 grand. But clearly there are some who are rich enough and nostalgic enough to pay a hundred times more than is necessary to buy a camera of comparable photographic quality today.

Those on the political left, for whom indignation is a way of life, are deeply offended by such frivolous expenditures by the rich. Congressman Dick Gephardt or Congressman David Bonior could no doubt produce several sermonettes on the subject. But the great Supreme Court justice Oliver Wendell Holmes said that the real cost of the rich to the rest of society is what they consume. How much is it costing the rest of us that some old-money heir or heiress, or some new Silicon Valley millionaire in his twenties, is splurging on this half-century-old camera that practically nobody else wants?

Suppose instead that the rich wanted the same things that everybody else wanted. What if Bill Gates developed a fetish for meat and potatoes, and spent ten or twenty billion dollars collecting vast amounts of meat and potatoes in refrigerated warehouses? This would deprive many working families across America of food and drive up the price to others.

The more far out and off-the-wall the purchases of the rich are, the less anybody else is deprived. When some rare stamp or antique piece of furniture is auctioned off for a small fortune at Sotheby's, it is no skin off anybody else's nose. To me, antiques are just old furniture and a stamp that won't get my letter where it is going is just a little piece of paper with some glue on it.

By definition, the rich can take all the serious necessities of life for granted. In fact, so can millions of other Americans who are not rich. What is left for the rich to want? Stuff that gives them a sense of specialness or distinction.

Vanity is not the most attractive of human traits, but it is not the most harmful either. Nor is vanity confined to the rich. Young slum hoodlums who fight—or even kill—other kids to get their designer clothes or sneakers are doing the same thing, at a lot higher cost to others.

There was a time when the poor stole bread to feed their children. You could understand that. But today, when riots and looting sweep through some slum, food is left unmolested while the looters—supposedly "enraged" by some injustice—can be seen happily carrying off TV sets, fancy clothes and the like.

Ironically, what the rich are often praised for is likely to do more harm than what they are condemned for. Donating money to left-wing causes brings automatic approbation in the media, in academia and wherever else the intelligentsia hang out.

Buy up land and donate it for "open space" and an idle heir or heiress will be forgiven for all the money that some ancestor of theirs earned by providing goods and services to millions. But this is much more like buying up meat and potatoes than it is like blowing 40 grand on an old camera.

The less land is available to build on, the more people are going to be crowded in the remaining land that is available—and the higher rents are going to be on that land. Should people packed into slums be grateful that the actions of the rich are driving up their rents and preventing them from getting a little elbow room in what the anointed like to call "urban sprawl"?

Then there are those rich people who bankrolled all sorts of Communist-front and fellow-traveler movements during the Cold War. How many people in the Gulags do you suppose felt the same glow of appreciation for their open mindedness and moral equivalence that was felt in Hollywood or Martha's Vineyard?

Some rich Silicon Valley entrepreneurs like to "give back" by literally serving food to the homeless. In other words, they are showing their gratitude to American society by subsidizing the lifestyle of people who refuse to work, in an economy with millions of unfilled jobs, and who carry out all sorts of anti-social or even criminal behavior on the streets.

All in all, the vanities and vices of the rich may do far less harm than their supposed virtues. Idle self-indulgence may not be pretty, but if it keeps the rich off the streets and out of mischief, so be it.

PERENNIAL
ECONOMIC
FALLACIES

Every time some new income statistics come out, two predictable fallacies follow in their wake. The first is that the rich are getting richer, while the poor are falling behind. The second is that the real income of American families has not risen significantly for years.

These fallacies return as regularly as the swallows returning to Capistrano, though not nearly as gracefully. A typical headline in the *New York Times* proclaims: "In A Time of Plenty, The Poor Are Still Poor." Yet study after study has shown that "the poor" do not remain poor in contemporary America.

An absolute majority of the people who were in the bottom 20 percent in 1975 have also been in the top 20 percent at some time since then. Most Americans don't stay put in any income bracket. At different times, they are both "rich" and "poor"—as these terms are recklessly thrown around in the media. Most of those who are called "the rich" are just middle-class people whose taxes the politicians avoid cutting by giving them that name.

There are of course some people who remain permanently in the bottom 20 percent. But such people constitute less than one percent of the American population, according to data published by the Federal Reserve Bank of Dallas in its 1995 annual report. Perhaps the intelligentsia and the politicians have been too busy waxing indignant to be bothered by anything so mundane as facts.

Alarmists are not talking about real flesh and blood people. They are talking about abstract categories like the top or bottom 10 percent or 20 percent of families or households. So long as all incomes are not identical, there will always be top and bottom 10 percents or 20 percents or any other percents. But these abstract categories do not contain the same people over time.

Households do not contain the same numbers of people, even at a given time. The bottom 20 percent of households contains 39 million people, while the top 20 percent contains 64 million. Comparing households is comparing apples and oranges.

If you are serious about considering the well-being of flesh and blood human beings, then you can talk about their real income per capita. But alarmists avoid that like the plague, because it would expose their little game for the fraud that it is.

Real income per capita has risen 50 percent over the same span of time when household income has remained virtually unchanged. How is this possible? Because households are getting smaller. The very fact that there are higher incomes enables more people to afford to go out and set up their own independent households.

Behind both the statistics on inequality that are spotlighted and the statistics on ever-changing personal incomes that are ignored is the simple fact that people just starting out in their careers usually do not make as much money as they will later on, after they have had years of experience.

Who should be surprised that 60-year-olds have higher incomes and more wealth than 30-year-olds? Moreover, that was also true 30 years ago, when today's 60-year-olds were just

30. But these are not different classes of people. They are the same people at different stages of their lives.

At some times and places, there have been whole classes of people who lived permanently in poverty or in luxury. But, in the United States today, the percentage of Americans who fit either description does not reach beyond single digits.

It is one thing to be concerned about the fate of flesh and blood human beings. It is something very different to create alarms about statistical relationships between abstract categories.

Despite desperate efforts of activists to keep "hunger in America" alive as an issue by manipulating numbers, actual examinations of flesh and blood people show no nutritional differences between people in different income brackets. In contrast to the gaunt and undernourished poor of other times and places, Americans in the lower income brackets today are slightly more likely to be overweight than is the rest of the population.

The magnitude of statistical differences may tell very little about the condition of human beings. A two-to-one difference in the amount of food available would be very painful if it meant that those on the short end did not have enough to eat. But a thousand-to-one difference in price between wearing a Rolex and wearing a Timex is something that can be left to the alarmists—especially since both watches tell time with about the same accuracy. And both are a lot more accurate than "income disparity" hysteria.

SWEATSHOPS
AT HOME
AND ABROAD

It is truly ironic that people at colleges and universities across the country have been organizing to protest sweatshop labor in the Third World, when the greatest examples of sweatshop labor in America are on their own campuses.

Where else can a nationwide cartel work people for no money at all, while collecting millions of dollars from the fruits of their labor? That cartel is the National Collegiate Athletic Association (NCAA) and the people whose work brings in millions at the gate are the athletes who play on college teams.

In big-time college football and basketball, it is not uncommon for the coach to make more money than the college or university president—sometimes several times what the academic chief executive makes. But if any money finds its way into the hands of the players who put their bodies on the line, that is called a "scandal."

One football player who put his body on the line and is now paralyzed as a result of an injury sustained during a game, Kent Waldrup, Jr., of Texas Christian University, was recently denied any right to disability benefits from the university by an appellate court because he was not an "employee."

The academic aspect of campus life is not a lot better, as far as sweatshop labor is concerned. Teaching assistants across the country are joining labor unions to try to get better pay for their work. Parents who pay megabucks tuition for their children to go to big-name colleges and universities may not realize that their offspring are all too often being taught by no-name teaching assistants who are paid a pittance, rather than by the big-name professors who give the institution its aura and collect six-figure salaries.

Teaching assistants do not simply assist with teaching. They teach many of the courses all by themselves. In some departments, more classes are taught by TAs than by professors. These include some of the top-rated universities in the country.

With both college athletes and TAs, the claim is made that they are being compensated by getting an education. Only for the TAs is that likely to be true in most cases. Big-time football and basketball are full-time jobs. Athletes have to go through the motions of getting an education, for the sake of appearances and eligibility to play. But those who actually get a degree—much less an education—are the exceptions, rather than the rule.

Teaching assistants are usually graduate students who are working toward their Master's degrees or their Ph.D.s, while taking on the job of teaching undergraduate courses that their professors don't want to be bothered teaching. In a big-name university, anyone taking introductory courses in math or English is very unlikely to see a member of the faculty standing in front of the class.

Graduate students in general are very vulnerable, since their first opportunities in the professional careers ahead of them depend on the recommendations of their professors, some of whom have exploited that dependency unconscionably. Some professors have stolen their graduate students' ideas and published them as their own. Others have exploited their graduate students sexually.

One professor at Stanford was accused of having sexually molested the son of one of his graduate students and committed suicide shortly thereafter. Most, however, pay no such price—or any price at all. Even the accused molester had a medal struck in his honor after his death.

If the morally anointed on campus want to protest exploitation, they need not look overseas—or even beyond their own ivy-covered buildings.

As for the people in the Third World, jobs with American companies operating there are likely to be among the best jobs available, even if these jobs don't pay as much as they pay in the United States. Since the workers are unlikely to produce as much output per hour as American workers, pressuring companies to pay American wages means that fewer Third World workers will have jobs at all.

If the real purpose of all the uproar about sweatshop labor in the Third World is to allow college students and professors to feel morally one-up on businesses that are providing much-needed jobs in poor countries, then it accomplishes that purpose. But it may accomplish nothing else, except perhaps to demonstrate yet again academic hypocrisy.

SANITY
IN
SAN FRANCISCO

Congratulations are in order for the *San Francisco Weekly*, for an informative article that introduces sanity into a subject where insanity is the norm—namely, rent control in San Francisco.

What has happened under stringent rent control laws in the city by the bay is what has happened in virtually every other city around the world where such laws have been passed. But it will still be news to rent control advocates, who seldom bother to get the facts.

According to the *San Francisco Weekly*, new construction of multifamily housing dropped by 32 percent within a decade after the city's rent control law was passed in 1979. Over the past ten years, the number of rental units in the city has declined absolutely by 7,500. The vacancy rate is below one percent. Nor has rent control meant low rents. The average rent for a one-bedroom apartment in San Francisco is nearly $2,000 a month.

None of this is unique to San Francisco. A study of 16 cities by William Tucker of the Cato Institute showed "that the advertised rents of available apartments in rent-regulated cities are dramatically higher than they are in cities without rent control." In view of this, it is not surprising that he also found homelessness more prevalent in cities with rent control.

How can this be, when the whole purpose of rent control is to keep rents down? First of all, the purpose of any policy tells you absolutely nothing about what will actually happen under that policy. Too many disastrous laws get passed because those who pass them win political points for their good intentions and nobody bothers to check up later to see what actually happened.

The San Francisco Board of Supervisors has recently commissioned the first official study ever done of the effects of rent control in the city. Imagine! The first rent control law was passed in 1979 and has been amended more than 50 times in the two decades since then—usually tightening the controls—but nobody in government has yet bothered to find out what the actual effect has been.

Politics is not about empirical realities, but about popular images. So long as the image of rent control is good, it wins votes at election time—and that is what it is all about, as far as politicians are concerned. Meanwhile, there is a whole movement of rent-control activists and tenants' rights advocates who say things like, "Housing is not a commodity." Mindless mantras like that make them look and feel like the morally anointed, and apparently that is good enough for them. Who needs facts when you have myths that serve your purposes?

The biggest myth is that rent control helps the poor. It does help those poor people who happen to have an apartment when rent control laws are passed—but it also helps the affluent and even the rich who happen to be on the inside looking out. However, as the housing supply dries up, who gets left out? The homeless people on the streets are certainly not the rich.

Studies in both Cambridge, Massachusetts and Berkeley, California showed that "rent-controlled apartments were concentrated among highly educated professionals." In New

York, people living in rent-controlled apartments have included the president of the New York Stock Exchange and even Hollywood stars who keep such apartments to use when they happen to be in town.

San Francisco's rent-control law, like those in other cities, was passed as a "temporary" measure to deal with some immediate crisis—in this case, the runaway inflation of the late 1970s. A cynic once said that there is nothing more permanent than a temporary government policy. Rent control laws were also passed as "temporary" measures in London and Paris during the First World War—and remained in force on past the Second World War.

Since there are always more tenants than landlords, and more people who don't understand economics than people who do, it is nearly impossible to get the voters in a community with rent control to vote it out. However, many state legislatures across the country have taken that decision out of local hands by passing laws forbidding cities and towns from having rent control. When rent control was gotten rid of this way in Massachusetts, new housing began to be built in formerly rent-controlled communities for the first time in decades.

It can be done. But it is unlikely to be done in San Francisco. Nor is the liberal state legislature likely to act. There is in fact a measure on this year's ballot to tighten rent control in San Francisco some more.

THE END OF MONTGOMERY WARD

The passing of a once-great business is often a time for nostalgia and regret, so the announced closing down of Montgomery Ward has provoked much media comment along these lines. But both the rise and the fall of Montgomery Ward illustrate the dynamic adjustments of a free market economy and the prosperity that it makes possible.

Although most people today think of Montgomery Ward as a chain of department stores, the company was one of the dominant retailers in the country for more than half a century before it opened its first store. It began as a mail-order house in 1872, when the United States was a rural country, with very high costs of delivering goods to a widely scattered population. Neither trucks nor automobiles nor airplanes had yet arrived on the scene, so transportation costs added greatly to the cost of getting merchandise to small general stores in isolated communities.

Montgomery Ward mailed its merchandise, lowering delivery costs by using the most efficient transportation available at the time—the railroad—and the only nationwide delivery service, the U.S. mails. Railroad tracks ran right through the huge Montgomery Ward warehouse in Chicago. The net result was that it could charge lower prices than others who used more costly methods of transportation, enabling more Americans to afford more things.

But nothing stays the same. Montgomery Ward was the largest retailer in the world in the 19th century, but that was destined to change because of a young railroad agent who sold watches on the side. His name was Richard Sears.

The company that Sears set up also grew into a mail-order house—one that eventually surpassed Montgomery Ward. Meanwhile, the country itself was changing. By 1920, there were for the first time more Americans living in urban areas than in rural areas. That changed the whole economics of retailing.

Now the cheapest way to deliver merchandise to many Americans was by setting up chains of stores where they lived. But neither Sears nor Montgomery Ward had any stores—nor any desire to build stores. They had been highly successful for decades in the mail-order business. Why change? When an executive at Montgomery Ward suggested to the head man that they start opening stores to supplement their mail-order business, he was fired for his trouble.

The greatness of a free-market economy is that it does not depend upon the wisdom of those who happen to be on top at the moment. The rich and complacent men who ran Montgomery Ward and Sears were destined to be forced into change by a new man named James Cash Penney, born and raised in poverty.

Penney's first experience as a retailer came as a one-third owner of a small store in a little town in Wyoming. Yet his ideas on retailing changed the whole industry. By 1920, there were 300 J. C. Penney stores—prospering, growing and taking business away from Sears and Montgomery Ward, both of which began losing millions of dollars. Only then did Sears begin to listen to the executive who had been fired from

Montgomery Ward and start opening its own stores, saving the company from the brink of bankruptcy.

Montgomery Ward then belatedly followed suit. The rich men who ran these two giant mail-order houses realized that they would not be rich much longer if they kept losing millions of dollars a year.

In the years after the Second World War, as the country grew more prosperous and people began moving to the suburbs, some Montgomery Ward executives suggested to the head man that they should start building stores in suburban shopping malls. They were fired for their trouble.

The net result was that Sears hit the shopping malls first and Montgomery Ward never caught up. Meanwhile, a young clerk in a J. C. Penney store—a man named Sam Walton— began learning retailing from the ground up. Later, he put his knowledge and insights to work in his own stores, which would eventually become the Wal-Mart chain, with sales larger than those of Sears and J. C. Penney combined.

Montgomery Ward once made a great contribution to the rising standard of living of ordinary Americans. But the continued prosperity of Americans eventually required that it be replaced by new businesses, better adapted to new conditions. Those who complain that some are "left behind" amid growing prosperity do not understand that leaving some behind is the way the country moves ahead.

"SAVING" SOCIAL SECURITY

Nothing seems so insecure as Social Security. However, before we start "saving" Social Security, we need to stop and think about why it needs saving in the first place. Then maybe we can avoid making the same mistakes all over again.

Some people blame the problem on the large numbers of "baby boomers" who will be retiring in the next few decades. But why don't we hear about private annuities that are worried about the number of baby boomers who will be retiring?

Social Security's problems go much deeper than the size of the generation that is going to be retiring. In fact, Social Security's problems go all the way back to the beginning—to the way it was set up, to the lies that politicians told about it and to the misconceptions and political irresponsibility that have now come home to roost.

Private insurance companies aren't panicked about the annuities they are going to have to pay to baby boomers because insurance companies operate in an entirely different way from Social Security. Insurance companies take their customers' premiums and invest them to create real wealth. Later, the earnings from that wealth can be used to pay annuities or life insurance benefits whenever they become due.

For example, if an insurance company uses its customers' premiums to build an apartment complex, then the rents coming in from those who live in the apartments can be used to pay the annuities or insurance benefits owed to those whose premiums built the buildings. The size of the previous generation or the next generation doesn't matter.

The reason it matters under Social Security is that there has never been any real wealth created. The government has simply been robbing Peter to pay Paul. This worked great when the baby boomers were paying into the system and their money was being used to pay benefits to a much smaller generation that was retired.

Now it has become obvious to everyone that this game will not work any more when the huge baby boomer generation itself retires. There will not be enough people working to pay them all the benefits they were promised, unless Social Security taxes are raised by huge amounts. Otherwise, the government will have to welch on its commitments to the retirees.

The biggest lie about Social Security is that it is some kind of "insurance." But, unlike insurance premiums, Social Security taxes create no wealth. They are spent when they get to Washington, just like any other taxes. Paper transactions create the illusion of a Social Security "fund," but there is no corresponding real wealth created—no factories, farms or railroads.

The basic principle of Social Security is the same as that behind illegal pyramid schemes run by con men. The first people to put their money into pyramid schemes get repaid handsomely from the money received from others who join later. That is what attracts still more suckers and enables the con men to rip them off.

Since the first people to join the Social Security system were from the relatively small generation of the 1930s, their later retirement benefits were easily paid with the money received from the much larger baby boom generation. So long as the pyramid keeps expanding, things are great, but eventually the pyramid stops expanding and those who joined last get left holding the bag.

That is why pyramid schemes are illegal and that is why Social Security is now in trouble. It is not because of some demographic fluke. It was a demographic fluke that kept it from collapsing before now.

It was the deceptions and irresponsibility of politicians that got us into this mess. If you think the way to get out of it is to let politicians continue to guide Social Security in the future, then you have missed the point completely.

Investing the public's retirement money in the creation of real wealth is an essential part of any permanent fix. But, if that means letting politicians throw their weight around in the stock market, then this is truly putting the fox in charge of the hen house.

There are all sorts of sound financial institutions through which ordinary Americans can put their retirement money into the creation of real wealth, without having to pick individual stocks themselves. The time is long overdue to let them do it. The whole history of Social Security shows how important it is to keep politicians' hands off that money.

SOCIAL SECURITY VS. PRIVATIZATION

According to the unanimous preliminary report of the special commission appointed to look into Social Security, the amount of money coming into the system will be insufficient to pay out what was promised by 2016. By 2030, the choice will be to reduce Social Security benefits by about one-fourth or raise payroll taxes by about one-third. After that it gets worse.

Liberal Democrats, who have always been the biggest supporters of Social Security, have attacked the commission's conclusions. Congressman Richard Gephardt, for example, has denounced the report as "scare tactics" and said that the Social Security system faces no problems until its trust fund runs out in 2038.

When the money going out exceeds the money coming in, you are in trouble—and that happens in 2016. Those who try to push the fatal date off to 2038 are counting the money that Social Security has in its so-called trust fund. However, this "trust fund" exists only as a legal technicality, not as an economic reality.

When your Social Security taxes get to Washington, they are spent—right then and there. What preserves the illusion of a "trust fund" is that the Social Security system is given government bonds in exchange for the money that Congress takes and spends. But, no matter what kind of accounting sleight-of-hand you use, you cannot spend and save the same money.

Those bonds in the Social Security "trust fund" represent no tangible assets—not houses, not factories, not cars, not trains. They are promises that can be kept only by taxing future taxpayers.

What if the bonds in the Social Security "trust fund" had never existed? Economically, the situation would be exactly what it is now. After 2016, the government would have to either raise additional taxes or lower the benefits. The bonds serve only to fool the gullible or the uninformed.

The crucial difference between a 100 percent government-run retirement system like Social Security and one in which individuals can invest at least part of their own retirement money in the market is that the market represents real things. Private investment creates the enterprises and industries which generate real wealth, not just paper promises.

When you own a share of a company that is building houses, cars or computers, then your money is creating a larger real wealth—for the country and for yourself—than if Washington politicians were spending your Social Security taxes as fast as they reach the Beltway.

Representative Barbara Lee of Oakland is typical of Congressional Democrats in opposing the idea that younger workers should be allowed to invest part of their retirement money in the market, rather than in Social Security. She said: "Social Security is an insurance program, it's not an investment program. And no way should we want workers to have their benefits put at risk and put them at the whims of the stock market."

This is classic liberalism, starting with an utter ignorance or total disregard of economics. An "insurance program" is not something different from "an investment program." Real insurance companies invest the premiums they receive, precisely in order to have the money available to be able to pay off annuities or insurance claims when these become due.

But Representative Lee is half right: Social Security is not an investment program. People like Representative Lee can spend the Social Security money as fast as it gets to Washington, without investing anything to pay off future retirees. An insurance company executive who did that could find himself behind the walls of a federal prison. Barbara Lee, however, is only likely to find herself re-elected, as a reward for handing out goodies bought with the money that workers think is being put aside for their pensions.

You can see why liberal Congressmen don't want to see any of the trillions of dollars in Social Security pass out of their control. You can also see the arrogance of liberals who say that they don't want "workers to have their benefits put at risk." Nobody is going to invest those workers' money in the private sector except those workers themselves.

If workers prefer to invest in mutual funds to taking their chances with a Social Security system that may never pay them back what they paid in, who are liberals to tell them that they don't have a right to do that with their own money? The so-called "whims of the stock market" are nothing compared to the whims of politicians.

MINIMUM
JOURNALISM

A front-page story about minimum wages in the *Wall Street Journal* illustrates what is wrong with contemporary journalism as much as it illustrates anything about the minimum wage law. The first nine paragraphs deal with one individual who is wholly atypical of people earning the minimum wage. She is a 46-year-old single mother who works full-time.

Way back on page 10, we learn from a small chart that just over half the people earning the minimum wage are from 16 to 24 years of age. Just over half of the minimum wage earners are working part-time. Nevertheless, the atypical middle-aged single mother is now brought back into the story again and covered for an additional 13 paragraphs on an inside page.

Three out of four pictures of people under the heading "The Faces of Low-Wage Work" are women over 40, including one who is 76.

This is clever propaganda, but it is lousy journalism. People don't buy a newspaper in order to be deceived.

While the *Wall Street Journal* has one of the most intelligent editorial pages anywhere, some of its news stories on social issues—as distinguished from financial issues—are too often examples of the kind of mushy and even biased journalism that gives political correctness a bad name.

The politically correct party line on minimum wages is

that people cannot afford to raise their families on low pay, so the government has to force employers to provide "a living wage" for families. But the vast majority of people making minimum wages are youngsters just beginning their careers. They are not going to be flipping hamburgers or sweeping floors all their lives. Most have better sense than to have children that they cannot feed and house.

Yet the main focus of this long article is on a small minority who have a "minimum wage career." Our atypical middle-aged single mother is invoked once again: "In Ms. Williams' case, practically everyone she knows has been mired in such occupations their whole working lives." Is it supposed to be news that birds of a feather flock together?

Are we supposed to base national policy on one woman's experience? If we wanted to watch Oprah Winfrey, would we be reading the *Wall Street Journal*?

What about those minimum wage earners who are just passing through that income bracket on their way up? Most of the people in the bottom 20 percent of the income distribution—"the poor"—are also in the top 20 percent at some other point in their lives, when they are now counted among "the rich." Usually they are not poor the first time nor rich the second time, but such is the state of political rhetoric.

The reality of what happens to people over time gets far less attention than one middle-aged single mother working at a minimum wage job—and, incidentally, receiving government subsidies.

The minimum wage law is very cleverly misnamed. The real minimum wage is zero—and that is what many inexperienced and low-skilled people receive as a result of legislation that makes it illegal to pay them what they are currently worth to an employer.

Most economists have long recognized that minimum

wage laws increase unemployment among the least skilled, least experienced, and minority workers. With a little experience, these workers are likely to be worth more. But they cannot move up the ladder if they can't get on the ladder.

That is the real tragedy of the real minimum wage—zero. It is not just the money that these young people miss. It is the experience that can turn out to be far more valuable to them than the first paychecks they take home.

This is especially tragic in the Third World, where multinational corporations may be pressured into setting wages well above what the local labor market conditions would justify. This pressure often comes from self-righteous people back home who mount shrill demonstrations in the mistaken belief that they are helping poor people overseas.

Half a century ago, Professor Peter Bauer of the London School of Economics pointed out that "a striking feature of many under-developed countries is that money wages are maintained at high levels" while "large numbers are seeking but unable to find work." These people can least afford to get the minimum wage of zero, just so that their would-be saviors can feel noble, or so that labor unions in Europe or America can price them out of a job, in order to protect their own members' jobs.

MERIT
AND
MONEY

Some people may have found it an inspiring example of social conscience when various super-rich people, such as the Rockefellers, came out publicly against repealing the taxes that the federal government levies against the property left by people who have died. But it is a lot less than inspiring when you look at it in terms of how much damage death taxes do to others and how little damage such taxes do to the super-rich.

When you have hundreds of millions of dollars—or tens of billions of dollars, in the case of Bill Gates—you are never going to be able to spend it all on your own lifestyle in your own lifetime. So this wonderful-sounding defense of estate taxes will cost the super-rich nothing in their own lives. Moreover, even if the government were to confiscate three-quarters of their wealth upon their death, their heirs would still never have to work a day in their lives, because the remainder would still be so huge.

It is a very different story for an ordinary farmer or storekeeper or someone who owns a little automobile repair shop. What happens to what he has worked for and saved over a lifetime can make a huge difference to his widow and his orphaned children. By what right should what he has already paid taxes on be taxed yet again at a time when his family has just lost its breadwinner?

Or do right and wrong no longer matter? Can we just say magic words like "social justice" and start confiscating? That has been tried in a number of countries—and its consequences have ranged from counterproductive to catastrophic.

Forcing viable businesses out of business because the heirs cannot pay the estate taxes without selling off the assets is a loss to the country, as well as an unjust burden on the individuals concerned. Moreover, people have foresight and one of the reasons they work and sacrifice is to see that those who are dependent on them will be taken care of after they are gone. Destroying or undermining that incentive is sabotaging a virtue that is as important morally and politically as it is economically.

Those who want a society where everyone depends on government for their needs may be happy to see yet another blow struck against self-reliance. But no one else should be.

Talk about how various people have been "winners" in "the lottery of life" or have things that others don't have just because they "happen to have money" is part of the delegitimizing of property as a prelude to seizing it.

Luck certainly plays a very large role in all our lives. But we need to be very clear about what that role is. Very few people just "happen" to have money. Typically, they have it because their fellow human beings have voluntarily paid them for providing some goods or services, which are valued more than the money that is paid for them. It is not a zero-sum game. Both sides are better off because of it—and the whole society is better off when such transactions take place freely among free and independent people.

Who can better decide the value of the goods and services that someone has produced than the people who actually use those goods and services—and pay for them with their own hard-earned money?

Luck may well have played a role in enabling some people to provide valuable goods and services. Others might have been able to do the same if they had been raised by better parents, taught in better schools or chanced upon someone who pointed them in the right direction. But you are not going to change that by confiscating the fruits of productivity. All you are likely to do is reduce that productivity and undermine the virtues and attitudes that create prosperity and make a free society possible.

There seems to be some notion around that only purely individual merit can justify differences in income and wealth. But we are all huge beneficiaries of good fortune that we do not deserve. By what merit do we deserve to be living more than twice as long as the cave man and in greater safety, comfort, health and prosperity? We just happen to have been born in the right place at the right time. As Hamlet said, give every man what he deserves and who would escape a whipping?

The question is not what anybody deserves. The question is who is to take on the God-like role of deciding what everybody else deserves. You can talk about "social justice" all you want. But what death taxes boil down to is letting politicians take money from widows and orphans to pay for goodies that they will hand out to others, in order to buy votes to get reelected. That is not social justice or any other kind of justice.

PART II
RACIAL
ISSUES

ROUTINE
CRUELTY

In a world where the media are ready to magnify innocuous remarks or a minor problem into a trauma or a disaster, there is remarkably little attention being paid to cruelties routinely inflicted on children by our laws and our courts. That cruelty is ripping children away from the only home they have ever known, to be sent away—often far away—to be raised by strangers.

Such drastic action may be necessary when children have been abused or neglected, but kids have been seized from loving homes where there has never even been an accusation of abuse or neglect. As with so many irrational acts, race and political correctness are involved.

One of the children who is currently being threatened with this fate is a little boy in California named Santos, who may be sent off to live on an Indian reservation in Minnesota, among people he has never known, speaking a language he does not understand. Moreover, the single woman who is trying to adopt him there has said that she plans to put him in day care, which he has never been in before. He has been cared for at home by a married couple since he was 3 months old. He will be soon be 3 years old.

How could such an insane situation have arisen? Easy. It is

called the Indian Child Welfare Act. And it began, like so many catastrophes, with good intentions.

Back in 1978, Congress passed the Indian Child Welfare Act to prevent Indian children from being removed from their families and tribes by outside know-it-alls and social engineers. So far, so good. But, once a law is on the books, it means whatever the lawyers and the courts say it means. That is how little Santos got trapped in a nightmare.

Santos is part Indian, but neither he nor his biological parents has ever lived on a reservation or among an Indian tribe. When he was born and began suffering withdrawal because of his mother's cocaine addiction, the authorities took custody of him. He was put into a foster home with a Spanish-speaking couple whom he now regards as his parents and who want to adopt him.

Santos' biological mother has shown very little interest in him—and even that little bit of interest has not been reciprocated by Santos. He has hung up on her when she phoned and cried when she visited. The woman on an Indian reservation did not even know of Santos' existence until informed by the tribal council, which wants to claim him under the Indian Child Welfare Act. Six months later, she saw the little boy for the first time.

It gets worse. Two psychologists have become involved in the case. Shrink A has "spent approximately 10 minutes alone" with Santos, according to the California Court of Appeal in its ruling this past October 19th. She did not interview the couple with whom he has been living all this time, even though a Spanish-speaking social worker was available to enable her to converse with the boy's foster parents.

Nevertheless, Shrink A has decided that Santos would be better off being "moved to be with his tribe and his family" on a reservation in Minnesota. This strained definition of "family" is based on the fact that the woman on the reservation is a distant relative of his mother. Incidentally, Shrink A has never interviewed this distant relative either. Undaunted, Shrink A has said that Santos would not be "catastrophically damaged" by the change because Santos has not "bonded" with his foster parents, but has "bonded to his birth mother, who is unable to care for him." This strained definition of bonding is based on counting the time spent in his mother's womb, as well as the 9 days he spent with her after birth.

A second psychologist based his conclusions on what he had actually seen, rather than on such speculations. What he saw was that little Santos clings to his foster mother and became distressed when his foster father was asked to leave the room, crying "papa, papa." At another time, when Santos was with his foster father and Shrink B wanted to see the little boy alone, Santos became "clingy" with his foster father and "hugged him tightly while exclaiming 'papa, papa.'"

Little Santos has not yet been sent to Minnesota. The appellate court said that the "matter is remanded for further proceedings," which means a continuing cloud of uncertainty hanging over a little boy who has become a little pawn. How could anyone do this to him? Tragically, it has happened to many others.

LOSING
THE
RACE

Recently published studies have focused attention on the gap between the test scores of black and white school children. One study showed that the gap, which had been narrowing somewhat in years past, has now widened.

Gaps between racial or ethnic groups in academic performances are commonplace around the world, though some discussions of the black-white difference in America treat it as if it were something unique, requiring a unique explanation—whether that explanation is genes or discrimination. An entirely different explanation is offered by a black professor at the University of California at Berkeley, John H. McWhorter.

In a recently published book with the double-meaning title, *Losing the Race* (and the subtitle, "Self-Sabotage in Black America"), Professor McWhorter argues that most black students do not work as hard as white or Asian students, partly because the culture that they come from fails to give as high a priority to academic achievement and partly because many of their peers regard academic striving as "acting white." McWhorter's arguments are fuller and more subtle than this summary can be, but that is the gist of it.

Various other studies of time spent on homework, tough courses taken and other indicators of student effort support McWhorter's thesis. The examples he gives from his own experience teaching black, white and Asian students will ring true to anyone else who has taught all three. Yet there are other black academics, activists and politicians who denounce such candor as McWhorter shows, seeing it as washing blacks' dirty laundry in front of white people.

McWhorter, however, clearly considers it less important to protect the image of blacks than to promote the education and advancement of blacks by facing reality and doing something about it. One of the things he wants done is putting an end to excuses and to the whole victimhood mentality which spawns excuses. To those who point to the poverty among blacks or to the inadequacies of ghetto schools, he replies by citing data which show that Asian American youngsters from low-income families have better academic records than black youngsters from affluent families—and that these Asian American youngsters do better even when attending the same inadequate schools as blacks.

Such brutal truths are of course anathema to those who reject any internal factors among the explanations of lagging black achievements in education or elsewhere. In the longer view of history, McWhorter acknowledges the negative effects of external factors such as slavery, discrimination and poverty. But he refuses to go along with the current use of these external factors to excuse their own lack of effort on the part of those blacks who have grown up in affluent middle-class communities that are racially integrated.

Although initially a supporter of affirmative action, Professor McWhorter now regards it as having outlived its usefulness and become counter-productive. Its main harm to blacks is in reducing incentives to do their best. Here McWhorter uses himself as one of many examples, admitting that he never went all-out to do his best work in high school, because he knew that this would not be necessary in order for him to be admitted to a first-rate college. Similar effects of affirmative action have been found in other countries around the world.

One of the chilling chapters in *Losing the Race* covers the controversy over teaching "black English" in the Oakland schools. Because McWhorter publicly opposed this practice as educationally harmful—"depriving many black children of a ticket out of the ghetto"—he found himself denounced by many other blacks to whom "presenting a united front outweighs acknowledging fact." Worse, those preoccupied with this united front against whites assume that a black person who goes against the party line "could only be doing so as either a mistake or as active treachery."

It would of course never occur to such people that it is they who are betraying the interests of the race by being willing to sacrifice a whole generation of black children, rather then let themselves be embarrassed in the eyes of whites. Among those publicly denouncing McWhorter were individuals who privately agreed with him that "black English" was a bad idea.

This is one of a small but growing number of books which discuss racial issues honestly. It is about time.

REPARATIONS
FOR
SLAVERY?

The first thing to understand about the issue of reparations for slavery is that no money is going to be paid. The very people who are demanding reparations know that it is not going to happen.

Why then are they demanding something that they know they are not going to get? Because the demagogues themselves will benefit, even if nobody else does. Stirring up historic grievances pays off in publicity and votes.

Some are saying that Congress should at least issue an official apology for slavery. But slavery is not something you can apologize for, any more than you can apologize for murder. You apologize for accidentally stepping on someone's toes or for playing your TV too loud at night. But, if you have ever enslaved anybody, an apology is not going to cut it. And if you never enslaved anybody, then what are you apologizing for?

The very idea of apologizing for what somebody else did is meaningless, however fashionable it has become. A scholar once said that the great economist David Ricardo "was above the unctuous phrases that cost so little and yield such ample returns." Apparently many others are not.

The only thing that would give the idea of reparations for slavery even the appearance of rationality is an assumption of collective guilt, passed down from generation to generation. But, if we start operating on the principle that people alive today are responsible for what their ancestors did in centuries past, we will be adopting a principle that can tear any society apart, especially a multi-ethnic society like the United States.

Even if we were willing to go down that dangerous road, the facts of history do not square with the demand for reparations. Millions of immigrants arrived in this country from Europe, Asia and Latin America after slavery was over. Are their descendants guilty too and expected to pay out hard cash to redeem themselves?

Even during the era of slavery, most white people owned no slaves. Are their descendants supposed to pay for the descendants of those who did?

What about the effect of all this on today's black population? Is anyone made better off by being supplied with resentments and distractions from the task of developing the capabilities that pay off in a booming economy and a high-tech world? Whites may experience a passing annoyance over the reparations issue, but blacks—especially young blacks—can sustain more lasting damage from misallocating their time, attention and efforts.

Does anyone seriously suggest that blacks in America today would be better off if they were in Africa? If not, then what is the compensation for?

Sometimes it is claimed that slavery made a great contribution to the development of the American economy, from which other Americans benefitted, so that reparations would be like back pay. Although slaveowners benefitted from slavery, it is by no means obvious that there were net benefits to the economy as a whole, especially when you subtract the staggering costs of the Civil War.

Should the immoral gains of dead people be repaid by living people who are no better off than if slavery had never existed? The poorest region of the United States has long been the region in which slavery was concentrated. The same is true of Brazil—and was true of 18th century Europe. The world-wide track record of slavery as an economic system is bad. Slaveowners benefitted, but that is not saying that the economy as a whole benefitted.

The last desperate argument for reparations is that blacks have lower incomes and occupations than whites today because of the legacy of slavery. Do the people who say this seriously believe that black and white incomes and occupations would be the same if Africans had immigrated voluntarily to this country?

Scholars who have spent years studying racial and ethnic groups in countries around the world have yet to come up with a single country where all the different groups have the same incomes and occupations. Why would people from Africa be the lone exception on this planet? Groups everywhere differ too much in too many ways to have the same outcomes.

Slavery itself was not unique to Africans. The very word "slave" derives from the name of a European people—the Slavs, who were enslaved for centuries before the first African was brought to the Western Hemisphere. The tragic fact is that slavery existed all over the world, for thousands of years. Unfortunately, irresponsible demagogues have also existed for thousands of years.

THE LESSONS
OF
INDONESIA

Tragic as the lethal rioting in Indonesia has been, what is an additional tragedy for Americans is how few of us seem to have understood what went wrong there—and what could go wrong here.

While the media depict the riots as being directed against Indonesia's corrupt and despotic President Suharto, the biggest victims are in fact members of the Chinese minority in that country. It is their stores that are being looted and burned, and it is they who are being assaulted and killed.

One TV journalist on the scene referred to the Indonesian rioters as "the dispossessed." Yet the very pictures his cameraman was taking showed the rioters looking far less like an enraged proletariat rising up against oppression than like happy looters toting home television sets and other goodies stolen from shopping malls.

There are many legitimate grievances against the Suharto regime and that may be what set off the riots in the first place. But that is no reason to romanticize the ugly envy and resentment that Indonesians have long felt against the Chinese, who have not dispossessed them of anything.

Some find it strange and sinister that the Chinese, who are just 5 percent of the population of Indonesia own an estimated 80 percent of the capital of the country. But it is neither strange nor sinister.

The Chinese did not come in and take over the commerce and industry of Indonesia. The Chinese *created* most of that commerce and industry. It is no more strange that most of the capital in the country belongs to the Chinese than it is that most of the feathers in the world belong to birds. That is where feathers originate.

What is strange—and what may ultimately be sinister in its effects—is the blind dogma that any deviation from an even distribution of income, wealth, occupations or honors is both odd and a sign of something nefarious going on. In reality, such "disparate" statistics are common around the world and have been common in centuries past.

People from India once had a similar predominance in the businesses of much of East Africa—not because they took over these businesses but because they created them. So did the Jews in prewar Poland, the Germans in southern Brazil, the Ibos in northern Nigeria, the Italians in Buenos Aires, the Lebanese in West Africa . . . and on and on.

If we want to understand why the majority populations of these various places did not have the same entrepreneurship as these minorities, then we can talk about history and culture. But, if we are ignorant of such things, then we can at least avoid misleading everyone with romantic hogwash about "the dispossessed."

President Suharto and his family have used the power of government to create lucrative monopolies for themselves, as well as raking off graft from legitimate businesses. But it is very doubtful that the president's heavy-handed military forces are letting the masses burn and loot the Suharto enterprises.

In short, those who caused the present economic crisis in Indonesia are suffering few, if any, consequences while those who built up much of this country are scapegoats being treated as if they had torn it down. Politics has a way of turning everything upside down.

The economic crisis in Indonesia was created by the government's austerity program, which was imposed by the International Monetary Fund as a condition for giving a multibillion-dollar bailout. These IMF officials are thousands of miles away from the riots, in Washington, D.C.

The ultimate beneficiaries of the bailout are the international financiers who put big bucks into risky investments in Indonesia, secure in the knowledge that IMF bureaucrats would bail them out if things turned bad.

Why is the IMF so generous with money supplied by American and other taxpayers? Precisely because it is other people's money—and because handing out that money allows the IMF to wield global power and impose their pet notions on governments that are desperate for the bailout.

When you see rioting in Indonesia, you are seeing your tax dollars at work.

You are also seeing what can happen when a corrupt president is above the law.

BLACKS
AND
BOOTSTRAPS

One of the things I have been falsely accused of many times over the years is advising blacks to lift themselves up by their own bootstraps. But you can look through the 21 books, dozens of articles and hundreds of newspaper columns I have written without finding any such statement. That is because I am not in the business of giving advice to individuals and groups, but rather in the business of discussing public policy and trying to show where one policy is better than another.

It is considered the height of callousness to tell blacks to lift themselves up by their own bootstraps. But the cold historical fact is that most blacks did lift themselves out of poverty by their own bootstraps—before their political rescuers arrived on the scene with civil rights legislation in the 1960s or affirmative action policies in the 1970s.

As of 1940, 87 percent of black families lived below the official poverty line. This fell to 47 percent by 1960, without any major federal legislation on civil rights and before the rise and expansion of the welfare state under the Great Society programs of President Lyndon Johnson.

This decline in the poverty rate among blacks continued during the 1960s, dropping from 47 percent to 30 percent. But even this continuation of a trend already begun long before cannot all be attributed automatically to the new government

programs. Moreover, the first decade of affirmative action—
the 1970s—ended with the poverty rate among black families
at 29 percent. Even if that one percent decline was due to
affirmative action, it was not much.

The fact that an entirely different picture has been culti-
vated and spread throughout the media cannot change the
historical facts. What it can do—and has done—is make blacks
look like passive recipients of government beneficence, causing many whites to wonder why blacks can't advance on their
own, like other groups. Worse, it has convinced many blacks
themselves that their economic progress depends on government programs in general and affirmative action in particular.

It is undoubtedly true that the careers of black "leaders,"
politicians and community activists depend heavily on government programs. It is their ability to lobby for government
goodies that keeps such people in business and in the lime-
light. It was the breakdown of restrictions on black voting in
the South that caused a rapidly rising number of black elected
officials.

Even today, it is the politicizing of racial hype that enables
many black public figures to remain public figures and to ex-
tort money and concessions from private businesses by threatening to call them racists or organize boycotts if they don't
pony up. There is no question that the 1960s marked the decisive upturn in opportunity for race hustlers.

At one time, the aspirations of black leaders and the well-
being of the black population at large coincided, since both
were striving to end Jim Crow laws and other racial barriers.
But such coincidences do not last, either among blacks or
among other racial or ethnic groups in the United States or in
other countries.

"Leaders" have their own interests and agendas that they
push, even when the effects on those for whom they claim to

speak are detrimental. That is where we are today. Black leaders have a vested interest in black dependency—on them and on the government that they can try to influence.

Independent blacks who make it on their own are ignored as irrelevant or distracting. That is true not only of individuals, but also of institutions like all-black Dunbar High School in Washington, which for 85 years brought quality education to its students. Dunbar students exceeded national norms on IQ tests, years before the Supreme Court said that separate education was inherently unequal.

Dunbar was located within walking distance of the Supreme Court that essentially declared its existence impossible. Ironically, it was the political maneuvering following the historic desegregation decision of the High Court that ended Dunbar's long career as a quality institution and reduced it to just another failing ghetto school. But there are other quality black schools today—and they are still largely ignored today.

We have now reached the point where virtually everything that serves black "leaders"—dependency, grievance-hunting, racial hype and paranoia—are major disservices to the cause of advancing blacks, at a time when their opportunities have never been better.

"RACISM"
IN WORD
AND DEED

It has become all too common for some innocuous remark by a public figure to be seized upon and twisted to make it seem "racist," setting off loud denunciations by those who are in the business of loud denunciations. Meanwhile, actions and policies that do very real and very lasting harm to racial and ethnic minorities not only pass unchallenged, but are often engaged in by politicians who enjoy overwhelming support from minority voters.

There was virtually no comment from black leaders or the media when recently published census data showed that the black population of San Francisco had declined 15 percent between the 1990 census and the 2000 census. In San Mateo County, on the adjoining peninsula, the decline was 20 percent. In once predominantly black East Palo Alto, blacks are now a minority.

All of these are places firmly under the control of liberal Democrats, so no politically incorrect words are ever likely to be said about blacks in the communities from which they are being forced out. Yet any businessman whose hiring policies had such a "disparate impact" on minority employment would be liable to find himself hauled into court and charged with discrimination.

The point here is not to claim that the substantial reduction of the black population in the San Francisco Bay area is a result of racism. The point is that there is something happening whose net effect is to make it harder for blacks to live in places dominated by Democrats, who receive nine-tenths of their votes.

It is very doubtful that the policies which force blacks out of much of the San Francisco peninsula are racially motivated. The affluent liberal-left types who dominate the region would very likely accept a black family that wanted to buy a house costing half a million dollars and up, or rent an apartment at a couple of grand a month.

Even in the more precious high-end communities on the peninsula, a place could probably be found for those blacks who can afford to buy lots zoned for a minimum size of two acres and requiring room for four parking spaces on their property, in addition to whatever space is taken up by their swimming pools and stables for their horses. It is just that not many blacks are in the market for such housing.

While it is not necessary to charge racism, it is also not simply a happenstance that liberal Democrats are in control in California communities where sky-high housing prices have forced ordinary people—black or white—to move out. The political agenda of California's liberal Democrats has made housing unaffordable at the very time when their words constantly proclaim their desire for "affordable housing."

There was a time, about 30 years ago, when California's housing prices were not very different from housing prices in the rest of the country. Then a combination of environmental extremists and other liberal-left types became dominant in the state's Democratic Party, leading to innumerable and ingenious restrictions on the building of housing.

That was the point at which coastal California's housing prices left planet Earth and soared into outer space. Now people of average incomes, of whatever race, have to move to communities farther inland to find homes or apartments they can pay for. Some have to move so far inland that you can even find a Republican in office now and then.

Housing is just one of the areas where the black vote goes overwhelmingly to politicians whose policies are harmful to blacks. Even more harmful in the long run are failing public schools in the ghettos, where much of the next generation has its hopes of advancement destroyed before they can even get off the ground.

No group is more in favor of vouchers than blacks—and no one is more opposed to vouchers than the Democrats, including the Congressional Black Caucus. This doesn't mean that Democrats are racist. It is just that they need the support of the teachers' unions, and they are not going to get it if they vote for vouchers, whereas they can count on the votes of blacks regardless.

Under these conditions, who should be surprised that Democrats are ready to sacrifice another generation of black youngsters for the greater good of the teachers' unions?

Urban Renewal, policies artificially forcing up the price of food and many job-destroying policies promoted by Democrats all work against blacks. But these are only deeds, while words seem to be supreme in politics.

SWEEPING
SUCCESS
UNDER THE RUG

Recently I was surprised to learn of a highly successful black architect whose career began back in the 1920s, and of a black engineer and inventor from even further back, in the 1870s. With all the attention being given to various blacks during "Black History Month" and other such celebrations, it seemed strange to me that so little attention had been paid to these two men.

There has also been a remarkable lack of interest in some academically outstanding black schools, despite much political hand-wringing over the problems of black education. Put bluntly, some kinds of success seem to be swept under the rug, while other minor figures are inflated for the sake of racial breast-beating.

Why?

Let us begin with Paul Williams, a black man who became an architect in southern California in the 1920s, despite warnings from others that there was no market for a black architect. Few of his own people had the money to hire an architect and whites would prefer to hire a white architect. The 1920s were, after all, one of the periods of the resurgence of the Ku Klux Klan and its spread outside the South. Racism was big.

Nevertheless, Paul Williams studied to become an architect. His first job offers were so meager that he agreed to become an office boy at an architectural firm—with no salary, working just to get experience. Yet, after he started working, the company decided to pay him after all. Obviously, he must have impressed somebody.

Over the decades that followed, Williams impressed many people. Wealthy white businessmen began having him design both their businesses and their homes. So did movie stars like Cary Grant, Frank Sinatra, and Lucille Ball and Desi Arnaz. He also designed churches and other structures, and was part of the team of architects who designed the modernistic theme building at the Los Angeles International Airport.

An even more remarkable black man was Elijah McCoy, born in 1844, the son of escaped slaves. He lived in Canada but somehow made his way to Scotland, where he studied engineering. After returning to North America, McCoy invented a device which allowed machines to be oiled automatically while still running. Before, machinery either had to be shut down to be lubricated—which was costly in terms of lost production—or boys had to risk injury by oiling by hand while the machines were moving.

McCoy's invention was so successful that it had many imitators. None was as good, however, and buyers began to insist on getting "the real McCoy"—adding a new idiom to the language.

Why are these men much less celebrated than other blacks whose achievements were not as great?

What they did was an individual achievement and owed nothing to the civil rights movements or other political activity. More than that, they cast doubt on the whole vision of blacks as being held back solely by white racism and discrimination. Both men encountered prejudice and discrimination, but it didn't stop them.

Much the same story could be told of various black schools

which maintained high academic standards, even during the era of Jim Crow, when separate was seldom equal and very few of the supposed "prerequisites" of good education were available. Here again was an achievement that did not follow the script of black protests or other appeals to whites.

Paul Williams was candid enough to say that cultural deficiencies within the black community played a role in the economic and social lags of blacks. In other words, white racism was not the be-all and end-all excuse. Other independent black achievements suggest the same thing. That may be why they are swept under the rug, lest the great ideological bubble burst.

A black attorney once told me that, when he first entered law school, the black students there told him that a certain professor never gave blacks a higher grade than C. But this particular student decided that he just had to have the course that this professor taught and so he took his chances. After he received a grade of B+ he was surprised to find other black students being resentful toward him. He too had burst the bubble.

Egos, careers and massive government programs have all been based on a certain vision of race. Anything which threatens that vision is likely to be ignored or resented. But we need success and the lessons taught by success more than we need any political vision.

SORTING
BY
RACE

New York City is cracking down on taxi drivers who refuse to pick up black males. The mayor, the media and the intelligentsia are suddenly energized, as if this were some new problem that they just discovered.

As a black male, I have for years either rented a car or had somebody pick me up to drive me to places in New York where I had to go at night, because I was not about to stand around waiting for a taxi to pick me up. There were no problems getting taxis in the daytime in midtown Manhattan, but night is a different ball game.

Do I resent having to make special arrangements? Of course. Do I blame the cabbies? No.

Given the crime statistics, do I have a right to demand that taxi drivers risk their lives for my convenience? What am I going to say to the widows and orphans of dead cabbies? "Hey, I have to get to the Manhattan Institute to give a talk and don't feel like bothering with Hertz or Avis"? That would be a very hard sell, especially to the widows and orphans of *black* taxi drivers, who also pass up black males at night.

The tragic irony in all this is that things were not always this way. There was a time when my biggest problem with taxis in New York was being able to afford one. Crime is the real culprit, however much the demagogues may prefer "racism." Do the cabbies suddenly become racists after sundown?

Professor David Levering Lewis' great book about the 1920s, *When Harlem Was In Vogue*, refers to taxis available there at night and being hailed by whites from downtown after they emerged from Harlem parties in the wee hours of the morning. That was a different world. The reality was different, not just "perceptions."

Racial profiling by the government is more troubling, especially when it involves armed police in broad daylight. But nobody judges each person as an individual, no matter how much that pious phrase is used. And race is by no means the only basis for profiling.

People familiar with the stringent security system that you have to pass through going into and out of Israel are amazed when I tell them that my wife and I have been through it four times without ever having our suitcases opened for inspection. For whatever reason, we must not fit the profiles used by Israeli security guards.

The last time we were going to Israel, we saw some poor lady right ahead of us held up for more than half an hour while the security guard opened up her suitcase and spread her belongings all over the counter. When our turn came, he waved us on impatiently, as if he didn't want to waste time on us.

Back when I was a young Marine who had graduated from the Navy's photography school at Pensacola, a group of us were assigned to the photo lab at Camp Lejeune, N.C. We were a bunch of cocky young guys who got a reputation as troublemakers and became known—not always affectionately—as "the Pensacola gang."

When the captain in charge had about as much of us as he could stand, he had us all transferred out—and separated.

Months later, another graduate from Pensacola was assigned to the lab but, the moment he set foot on the base, he was told that his orders had been changed. He was transferred sight unseen.

He was not judged as an individual. Just the one word "Pensacola" probably sent the captain's blood pressure up through the roof. Except for me, all these people were white, so race had nothing to do with it. But it was profiling.

The new guy, a very easy-going fellow who would undoubtedly have fit in well at the lab, had a right to be resentful. But toward whom? Just the captain or also those Pensacola graduates who preceded him?

An even more personal example involved a physician who referred me to a cardiologist for extraordinary testing after he had given me a routine physical. The physician said that nothing he had seen in his examination of me would have led him to refer me to a cardiologist. He did it because three of my brothers had died of heart attacks. I was not judged as an individual—nor should I have been.

We ought to be concerned because taxis avoid picking up black males at night. But we ought to be concerned about what causes it, not just seize another opportunity for self-righteous denunciation.

THE
MAGIC
WORD

Perhaps Secretary of State Colin Powell's decision to pull the American delegation out of the so-called U.N. World Conference Against Racism in Durban, South Africa, will be just a footnote in history. But we can at least hope that it may be a turning point toward a future time when "racism" will no longer be a magic word used to gain money or political concessions.

Within the United States, Jesse Jackson and others have repeatedly scared millions of dollars out of big corporations, just by threatening to use the magic word "racism." Even the police have sometimes turned a blind eye to violations of the law, lest they be tarred with that magic word that will bring the whole liberal media crashing down on them. But letting criminal activity go on unimpeded and unpunished has hurt minority communities most of all.

Against this background, it was to be expected that some African and Arab nations would hope that invoking this magic word might scare some money out of the United States as "reparations" for slavery and get some kind of United Nations condemnation of Israel as a bonus. But this time the magic didn't work.

Singling out Israel to blame for the Middle East's problems was probably the straw that broke the camel's back, leading both the U.S. and Israel to withdraw their delegations from the conference in Durban. Arab caricatures of Jews with big noses and bloody fangs were hardly a way of being against racism.

The real world-class chutzpah, however, was the demand of African and Arab nations for reparations of slavery. Just who do you suppose enslaved the millions of Africans who ended up in the Western Hemisphere? It was the Africans. And who enslaved the even greater number of millions of African slaves who ended up in the Islamic world? It was the Arabs.

During the era of African slavery, Europeans died like flies in tropical Africa, where diseases flourished for which they had no biological immunity and for which medical science had yet to devise a cure. Capturing people to sell into slavery was the work of Africans in West Africa and of Arabs and Africans in East Africa.

Europeans came in their ships, bought slaves from the Africans, and then left the scene quickly before they fell sick from African diseases. Even so, many white crewmen on the ships bringing slaves from Africa to the Western Hemisphere died on the way. The notion that it was white people who introduced slavery to Africa, or who captured most of the slaves themselves, may fit the mindset of those who thought that *Roots* was history, but this myth will not stand up to facts, logic or economics.

Since it was the Africans and the Arabs who actually caught and sold slaves, do the African and Arab nations plan to send reparations over here to the descendants of enslaved Africans living in the Western Hemisphere? Of course not. They want the United States to lay some of those American dollars on them! We have fallen for so many other sucker plays in the past, why not try this one on us?

When slavery is mentioned, too many people automatically think of whites enslaving blacks. That is not even one-tenth of the story of slavery, which existed on every inhabited continent. The very word "slave" derives from the word for some white people who were enslaved on a mass scale—the Slavs—for more centuries than blacks were enslaved in the Western Hemisphere.

Moreover, slavery existed in the Western Hemisphere before the first black or white person ever set foot on these shores. The indigenous peoples of this hemisphere enslaved one another, just as Asians enslaved Asians, Europeans enslaved Europeans, and Africans enslaved Africans. Attempts to limit the discussion of slavery to slavery in the United States or in Western civilization make sense only as a strategy to get money or political concessions.

Western civilization was the first civilization to regard slavery as morally wrong and it is the civilization with the most sense of guilt about it. To this very moment slavery continues in parts of Africa and the Islamic world. Very little noise is made about it by those who denounce the slavery of the past in the West, because there is no money to be made denouncing it and no political advantages to be gained.

If the American delegation walking out of the U.N. Conference Against Racism represented a belated waking up to the scams being played, that could be a very healthy sign for the future—not only on the international scene, but within the United States as well.

RACE
AND THE
NEW CENTURY

W. F. B. DuBois once said that the problem of the 20th century world was going to be the problem of the color line. Like many ringing predictions, it missed the mark by a wide margin. The biggest atrocity of this century against any people—the Holocaust—involved people of the same color as those who killed them. So do the current atrocities in the Balkans and in Africa.

In one sense, however, DuBois was right. The biggest political problem of this century for black Americans has been the fight to abolish the color line, epitomized by Jim Crow laws in the South.

With a new century approaching, it is by no means clear that the biggest problem facing black Americans is still the problem of the color line. Indeed, that problem has already been superseded by another: self-destruction, both cultural and physical.

In the high-tech world that is already upon us and shows every sign of expanding dramatically in the next century, know-how is king. People who started businesses in garages have gone on to earn fortunes because they had the know-how. You don't even have to find someone to hire you. You can start up your own business.

People from India are not only hired in Silicon Valley, they own their own companies in Silicon Valley. So much for the color line. But you have to have the know-how. And even college-educated blacks are seldom going into the fields where you can get high-tech know-how. Ghetto schools seldom provide the skills on which science and engineering are based.

The public schools are where the battle needs to be fought, but too many black political "leaders" are too dependent on labor unions in general and the teachers union in particular to fight that battle. And they are too dependent on a vision of victimhood to risk telling young blacks that they have to get their own act together too.

On the contrary, Jesse Jackson is currently defending hoodlums who have been expelled from school. This is a classic example of black "leaders" who are leading their people to cultural suicide, just as surely as cult leader Jim Jones led his followers to physical suicide in Guiana. There are few things more dishonorable than misleading the young.

It is an old cliche that generals try to fight the last war over again. That is what a whole generation of black "leaders" is doing—fighting the old war against the color line. Jesse Jackson's claim that blacks are shut out of Silicon Valley jobs is that old war—as well as a lie. Blacks with the technical know-how already own their own businesses in Silicon Valley.

Fortunately, Silicon Valley CEO T. J. Rodgers challenged Jackson to a public debate on the issue—and Jesse backed out. Too many other CEOs in too many other corporations find it easier to pay off Jesse Jackson and other hustlers. That may be the path of least resistance for these corporations, but it is a disservice to America, including black America.

It has been said that the truth will set you free. In the present situation, the truth is the only thing that will set young blacks free. So long as a whole generation of young blacks continues to be told, day in and day out, that their problems are caused by whites, they are never going to be prepared to take advantage of the opportunities in Silicon Valley or anywhere else.

Many of those who still push the old party line on race also try to get young blacks to study hard in school and prepare themselves for the opportunities available. But mixed messages don't hack it.

All across the country, there are heartbreaking stories about young blacks in schools who condemn those among them who try to be good students as "acting white." Sometimes the condemnation extends to ostracism and beyond—to outright violence.

Many blacks who are sending mixed messages to the young are horrified at such attitudes. But there is no point creating the cause and then being appalled at the effect.

Perhaps the biggest problem of the 21st century will be moving on beyond the problems of the 20th century to confront the new realities—and the new opportunities. But that may require a whole new generation of black leaders to arise, no longer looking back at the struggles of the 1960s but ahead to the demands of a very different world.

That takes time. But it ought to start now.

"ACCESS"
TO
RESPONSIBILITY

Dishonesty has become so routine in discussions of racial issues that perhaps I should not have been surprised at a headline in the *San Francisco Chronicle* that read: "Minority Students Need Access to Honors Classes."

Are there honors classes which refuse to accept minority students who meet the same standards as others? If so, that should be the subject of a lawsuit, not a mere op-ed piece. But, of course, this is not the case.

"Access" is one of the great dishonest words of our times. I have had as much access to a career in professional basketball as Michael Jordan had. He just happened to play the game a lot better. Indeed, practically everybody has played the game a lot better than I did.

My problem was not "access" to basketball. Neither is the problem access in most other situations in which this slippery word is used politically. At the very least, we need to distinguish access from performance.

Blurring that distinction is at the heart of many claims of discrimination based on statistics. The claim behind the misleading headline in the *Chronicle* is that the University of California system is discriminating against black and Hispanic students who apply—by judging them by the same standards applied to others!

One of the factors taken into account in admissions decisions in the University of California system is a grade-point average that gives extra points for grades earned in honors courses. High schools in predominantly black and Hispanic neighborhoods offer fewer honors courses. Therefore, the lawsuit claims, the admissions criteria are discriminatory.

If this argument were meant seriously, instead of politically, then the remedy would be to have high schools in black and Hispanic neighborhoods offer more honors courses. If anybody should be sued, then it should be the public schools, rather than the University of California, which has nothing to do with how many honors courses are or are not taught in various high schools.

The real point of the lawsuit, and of the op-ed support of it, is to get the admissions standards repealed or circumvented, so that there will be a larger body count of so-called "underrepresented minorities" on University of California campuses. If this effort is successful, blacks and Hispanics may not get any better education in high schools, but their symbolic presence will be greater at Berkeley, UCLA, etc.—even if they flunk out before graduating.

Use of the term "underrepresented minorities" is not accidental. It would be hard to make the case that white folks are keeping out non-whites, when Asian Americans are greatly over-represented among students in the University of California system, as they are in other top-level institutions around the country.

If the real problem is access, then why do the Asian American students happen to have it, while black and Hispanic students don't? You could turn the question around and ask: Why do blacks seem to have "access" to professional basketball, while Asian and Hispanic Americans seem not to?

The answer in both cases is the same: Access is not the issue. Performance is the issue.

You cannot have more honors classes in schools where students do not do honors-level work, unless you are prepared to define honors classes downward and have the term become meaningless. There is far too much research available on academic performance differences between Asian American students and students from "underrepresented minorities" for this simple, uncontested fact to be unknown to those who are accusing the University of California of "discrimination" for treating all applicants alike.

What are called "inequities in secondary education" could more accurately be called differences in the extent to which students are prepared to do the kinds of work required in honors courses. A case might be made that individual black or Hispanic students who are ready for honors work suffer from the fact that there may not be enough of their classmates who share their dedication.

There are various ways this problem might be dealt with—if one honestly wanted to deal with it, instead of using it to claim special exemptions from university admissions standards. But no such exemptions are likely to do nearly as much good for "underrepresented minorities" as "access" to personal responsibility.

PART III
POLITICAL ISSUES

POVERTY
AND
THE LEFT

The privations and sufferings of the poor have long been central themes in the vision of the political left. That is what attracted many of us to the left in our youth. But the actual consequences of the agenda of the left on the poor—and on others—is what eventually drove many of us to the right.

Most of the leading opponents of the left, in the United States and around the world, began on the left. These include Ronald Reagan, Milton Friedman and the whole neo-conservative movement, as well as Raymond Aron in France and Friedrich Hayek in Austria. There is no comparable exodus from the right to the left.

Why is this so? The favorite explanation by those who remain on the left is that their former comrades "sold out." But nobody sells out to the lowest bidder. The real money, for intellectuals at least, is overwhelmingly on the left. Black intellectuals, especially, can easily earn six-figure incomes just from lecture fees alone at colleges and universities around the country.

All it takes are some heated accusations of "racism" against whites and denunciations of American society in general, with perhaps a few antisemitic remarks thrown in for good measure. Nowhere can you make more money with less effort or ability. By contrast, there is very little demand for conservative speakers—black or white—on campus, and the few who show up are likely to be heckled or shouted down.

Nor are journalism or the arts havens for conservatives. Far from it. Whatever blacklist existed against Communists and their fellow-travelers in Hollywood during the McCarthy era, it has been completely outstripped by the blacklisting or intimidation of conservatives there now.

If the exodus from the left is not due to people selling out to the lowest bidder, then what does cause it?

Let us go back to the poor. Why are we concerned about them? Some are concerned lest the poor have inadequate food, shelter or other basic requirements for life. Others are concerned because of the inequalities, disparities or "gaps" that they represent. And still others are concerned because the poor can serve as a rationale for increasing the political power of the left.

Those who are primarily concerned about the well-being of the poor are likely to discover over time that much of the agenda of the left does not really do much good for the poor, and some of that agenda—environmental extremism, for example—actually makes the poor worse off.

Meanwhile, nothing has a track record of lifting millions of people from poverty to prosperity like a free market economy. Most officially "poor" Americans today have things that middle-class Americans of an earlier time could only dream about—including color TV, videocassette recorders, microwave ovens, and their own cars. Moreover, half of all poor households have air-conditioning.

Leftist redistribution of income could never accomplish that, because there are simply not enough rich people for their wealth to have such a dramatic effect on the living standards of the poor, even if it was all confiscated and redistributed. Moreover, many attempts at redistributing wealth in various countries around the world have ended up redistributing poverty.

After all, rich people can see the political handwriting on the wall, and can often take their money and leave the country, long before a government program can get started to confiscate it. They are also likely to take with them skills and entrepreneurial experience that are even harder to replace than the money.

For those of us whose main concern is the well-being of ordinary people, it is a no-brainer to abandon the left as soon as we acquire enough knowledge about what actually happens, as distinguished from what leftist theories say will happen.

It is a very different story for those on the left whose goal is either a self-righteous sense of superiority or the political power with which to express their self-infatuation by imposing their vision on others. Here the poor are a means to an end. These kinds of leftists show remarkably little interest in the creation of wealth, which has raised living standards for the poor, as compared to their obsession with redistribution, which has not.

These kinds of leftists concentrate on inequalities that can be dealt with by turning money and power over to people like themselves. These kinds of leftists will never desert the cause that serves them so well, no matter how badly it serves others.

"USEFUL IDIOTS"

Lenin is supposed to have referred to blind defenders and apologists for the Soviet Union in the Western democracies as "useful idiots." Yet even Lenin might have been surprised at how far these useful idiots would carry their partisanship in later years—including our own times.

Stalin's man-made famine in the Soviet Union during the 1930s killed more millions of people than Hitler killed in the Holocaust—and Mao's man-made famine in China killed more millions than died in the USSR. Yet we not only hear little or nothing about either of these staggering catastrophes in the Communist world today, very little was said about them in the Western democracies while they were going on. Indeed, many useful idiots denied that there were famines in the Soviet Union or in Communist China.

The most famous of these was the *New York Times'* Moscow correspondent, Walter Duranty, who won a Pulitzer prize for telling people what they wanted to hear, rather than what was actually happening. Duranty assured his readers that "there is no famine or actual starvation, nor is there likely to be." Moreover, he blamed reports to the contrary on "rumor factories" with anti-Soviet bias.

It was decades later before the first serious scholarly study of that famine was written, by Robert Conquest of the Hoover

Institution, always identified in politically correct circles as "right-wing." Yet when the Soviets' own statistics on the deaths during the famine were finally released, under Mikhail Gorbachev, they showed that the actual deaths exceeded even the millions estimated by Dr. Conquest.

Official statistics on the famine deaths in China under Mao have never been released, but knowledgeable estimates run upwards of 20 million people. Yet, even here, there were the same bland denials by sympathizers and fellow travellers in the West as during the earlier Soviet famine. One celebrated "expert" on China wrote: "I saw no starving people in China, nothing that looked like old-time famines." Horrifying as the pre-Communist famines were, they never killed as many people as Mao's famine did.

Today, even after the evidence of massive man-made famines in the Communist world, after Solzhenitsyn's revelations about the gulags and after the horrors of the killing fields of Cambodia, the useful idiots continue to deny or downplay staggering human tragedies under Communist dictatorships. Or else they engage in moral equivalence, as *Newsweek* editor and TV pundit Eleanor Clift did during the Elian Gonzalez controversy, when she said: "To be a poor child in Cuba may in many instances be better than being a poor child in Miami and I'm not going to condemn their lifestyle so gratuitously."

Apparently totalitarian dictatorship is just a lifestyle, like wearing sandals and beads and using herbal medicine. It apparently has not occurred to Eleanor Clift to ask why poor people in Miami do not put themselves and their children on flimsy boats, in a desperate effort to reach Cuba.

Elian Gonzalez and his mother were only the latest of millions of people to flee Communist dictatorships at the risk of their lives. Some were shot trying to get past the Berlin wall and hundreds of thousands of "boat people" were drowned trying to escape a Communist Vietnam that many useful idiots were celebrating from inside free democracies. Many who escaped from the Soviet Union to the West during the Second World War were sent back by American authorities, except for those who committed suicide rather than go back.

Yet none of this has really registered on a very large segment of the intelligentsia in the West. Nor are Western capitalists immune to the same blindness. The owner of the Baltimore Orioles announced that he would not hire baseball players who defect from Cuba, because this would be an "insult" to Castro. TV magnate Ted Turner has sponsored a TV mini-series on the Cold War that has often taken the moral-equivalence line.

Turner's instruction to the historian who put this series together was that he wanted no "triumphalism," meaning apparently no depiction of the triumph of democracy over Communism. Various scholars who have specialized in the study of Communist countries have criticized the distortions in this mini-series in a recently published book titled *CNN's Cold War Documentary*, edited by Arnold Beichman.

Meanwhile, that moral-equivalence mini-series is being spread through American schools from coast to coast, as if to turn our children into the useful idiots of the future.

FACTS
VERSUS DOGMA
ON GUNS

For years, the tragic shooting of President Reagan's press secretary James Brady has been exploited politically by gun-control advocates. Federal gun-control legislation has been called "the Brady bill." Yet there was scarcely a peep from the liberal media when it was announced recently that the man who shot Brady—John Hinkley—will be allowed furloughs from the mental hospital in which he has been kept.

Unfortunately, this is a classic liberal pattern—remarkably little concern over those particular people who actually commit crimes with guns, combined with ferocious crusades against law-abiding citizens who own firearms.

Furloughs, parole, probation or lenient sentences for violent criminals do not alarm the liberals. What alarms them is the thought that people who have never shot anybody might be able to have a gun in their home or business to protect themselves against the kinds of armed criminals that liberals allow to walk the streets.

Liberal dogma on gun control is like liberal dogma on so many other issues: Ordinary people cannot be trusted to look out for themselves, but must be put under the thumb of wiser and nobler people—such as liberals—through strict government regulations. According to the gun-control zealots, we will shoot each other in the heat of arguments if we have guns.

Automobile accidents will lead to gunfire between angry drivers.

In other words, innocent people cannot be trusted with firearms. Far better to leave them helpless against armed criminals.

It is bad enough that liberals have this vision of the world. What is worse is that the liberal media will consistently ignore or suppress any facts which contradict that vision.

A massive empirical study by John Lott of the University of Chicago Law School shows the direct opposite of virtually everything in the liberal vision of gun control. Rising rates of gun ownership in particular counties across the country have almost invariably been followed immediately by falling rates of violent crimes in those counties.

This should not be a surprise to anyone. Violent criminals prefer helpless victims, not people who can shoot them full of holes. But where have you seen this empirical study mentioned in the media? Its title is *More Guns, Less Crime.*

In those European countries where citizens almost never have guns, burglaries are far more common than in the United States, and the burglars do not spend nearly as much time casing the place before breaking in. Similarly, in those American communities where liberal politicians have long had tight control, law-abiding citizens are similarly disarmed and similarly vulnerable.

As for the gunplay that would supposedly follow every fender-bender on the highway, John Lott has been able to find only one example. Two truckers had an accident and one was giving a brutal, bone-breaking beating to the other, until the second trucker pulled out a gun and opened fire, probably saving his own life.

Even in counties where a high percentage of the people are armed, bullets are not flying hither and yon on the highways—or anywhere else. There are usually far more shootings in places where the criminals know that ordinary citizens are unlikely to be able to shoot back.

Isolated incidents of accidental death from guns are inevitable in a country of more than a quarter of a billion people, just as there are accidental deaths from swimming pools, ski runs, wild animals and other causes. But only accidental gunshot deaths are played up big in the media. The larger numbers of lives saved by armed citizens protecting themselves and their families are seldom reported, much less weighed against the isolated gunshot accidents.

If our concern is for the safety of decent, law-abiding people, then all the facts need to be considered. But nothing that undermines the gun-controllers' vision is likely to be reported when the mass media show more concern for protecting liberal dogma than for protecting people.

In the media, it is all presented as a story of humanitarian efforts by the good guys to save lives against the evil resistance of the National Rifle Association. In the media, James Brady is repeatedly put on the screen when the issue comes up. Meanwhile, the man who shot Brady gets furloughs and nobody cares.

GLOBAL
HOT
AIR

A new political dogma is being spun in the media. "Science," they say, has now "proved" that global warming is a real danger and that human beings are responsible for it, so that we need to take drastic steps to reduce greenhouse gasses. This has been the widespread response to a recent publication by the National Academy of Sciences, which many in the media have taken as proof that we need to follow the drastic requirements of the Kyoto accords, in order to reduce the threat of global warming.

There were some pretty heavy-weight scientists involved in the NAS discussions of the global warming issue. But, as the report itself stated clearly, these scientists not only did not write the report, they didn't even see it before it was published. They "were not asked to endorse the conclusions or recommendations nor did they see the final draft of the report before its release."

So much for "science" having "proved" global warming and its human causation. Scientists were used as window dressing for a report made by government officials. Moreover, even that report was unable to claim unanimity among scientists on the global warming issue, though some in the media seem to think that it did.

The stampede toward draconian changes in our economy

and in the whole American way of life is all too congenial to the mindset of the intelligentsia in general and the liberal media in particular. Anything that requires their superior wisdom and virtue to be imposed by government on the benighted masses has a favorable reception waiting in those quarters.

Back in the 1970s, the hysteria was about global cooling and the prospect of a new ice age. A National Academy of Sciences report back then led *Science* magazine to conclude in its March 1, 1975 issue that a long "ice age is a real possibility." According to the April 28, 1975 issue of *Newsweek*, "the earth's climate seems to be cooling down."

A note of urgency was part of the global cooling hysteria then as much as it is part of today's global warming hysteria. According to the February 1973 issue of *Science Digest*, "Once the freeze starts, it will be too late."

Nothing is easier than to come up with mathematical models and doomsday scenarios. Politicians and government bureaucrats have been trying for well over a decade to sell a doomsday scenario of global warming, which would enhance the power of—you guessed it—politicians and bureaucrats.

Among scientists specializing in the study of weather and climate, there are many differences of opinion, reflecting the complex and uncertain data. Among the prominent scientists who do not go along with the global warming hysteria are Richard S. Lindzen, who is professor of meteorology at MIT, and Dr. S. Fred Singer, who created the American weather satellite system and whose book, *Hot Talk, Cold Science*, is must reading for those who want scientific facts rather than a political stampede.

Although Professor Lindzen is one of the big names listed in the National Academy of Sciences report, he disagrees with the global warming hysteria. As Professor Lindzen notes, "the climate is always changing." Innumerable factors go into temperature changes and many of these factors, such as the changing amounts of heat put out by the sun during different eras, are beyond the control of human beings.

Certain gasses, such as carbon dioxide, have the potential to affect temperatures, but that is very different from saying that a particular rise in temperature during a particular era is necessarily due to "greenhouse gasses." A major part of the rising temperature over the past century took place before World War II—which was also before the large increase in carbon dioxide emissions in our time.

The National Academy of Sciences report itself tiptoes around the fact that the timing of temperature increases does not coincide with the timing of increases in greenhouse gasses. As the NAS report puts it: "The causes of these irregularities and the disparities in timing are not completely understood."

Even if we were to cripple our economy by carrying out the radical steps proposed in the Kyoto accords, this "would not result in a substantial reduction in global warming," according to Professor Lindzen. He laments the use of science "as a source of authority with which to bludgeon political opponents and propagandize uninformed citizens." Unfortunately, many of those uninformed citizens are in the media.

"CAMPAIGN
FINANCE REFORM"
FOLLIES

To crusaders for "campaign finance reform," as with many other political crusaders, the facts simply do not matter. What matters is their vision—and winning. Facts can be left to others.

Most of the arguments for campaign finance reform cannot stand up to the facts. Take the notion that, without government regulation of campaign contributions, people with big money will simply "buy the election." What are the facts?

The long list of rich people who became political candidates and lost, despite spending big bucks out of their own pockets, goes back as far as William Randolph Hearst and comes forward to Ross Perot and Steve Forbes. When the Republicans won control of the House of Representatives in 1994, for the first time in 40 years, the average winning Republican candidate spent less than the Democrat he defeated. Then, eight years later, when the Democrats staged a comeback and reduced the Republican majority, their spending averaged less than that of the Republicans.

What about the notion that the big money will always back conservative or pro-business candidates, giving one side of the political spectrum an unfair advantage at the polls? Big campaign money contributors have bankrolled political icons of the left from William Jennings Bryan to Bob LaFollette and Hiram Johnson in a bygone era to Eugene McCarthy and George McGovern in a later era. Hollywood millionaires were among Bill Clinton's biggest supporters and billionaire Ted Turner bankrolls left-wing causes.

What about the much-touted "quid pro quo" sought by "special interests"? Does this produce "the best politicians money can buy," as claimed by campaign finance crusaders? Here we run into a chicken and egg problem. Do contributors generally contribute to elected officials who already espouse positions they like or do the politicians take their positions in order to attract money?

Since there is money available on both sides of most issues, it is by no means an open and shut case that positions are generally taken just in order to attract money. A Congressman who votes in favor of drilling for oil in Alaska may get contributions from the oil industry but, if he voted to oppose oil drilling in Alaska, he could get money from the Sierra Club.

According to House minority leader Richard Gephardt: "What we have is two important values in direct conflict: freedom of speech and our desire for healthy campaigns in a healthy democracy." Whatever Congressman Gephardt's definition of a "healthy" campaign, it is not part of the Constitution of the United States—and free speech is.

Across a whole spectrum of institutions, free speech is being stifled so that the politically correct vision of the left can prevail, as it does in our educational system from the kindergarten to the graduate schools. It is the same story in most of the media. When a homosexual is murdered by anti-gay hoodlums, that is big news from coast to coast, but when two homosexuals capture, rape and kill a teenage boy, that story seldom sees the light of day.

Campaign finance restrictions reduce the chances of letting the public hear anything that has not been filtered through the liberal media and the liberal academic establishment.

What have been the actual consequences of previous campaign finance laws? A scholarly study of such laws—*Unfree Speech* by William A. Smith—concludes that they affect the channels through which money reaches political campaigns, rather than the total amount of money.

Lots of innocent people have been caught in legal technicalities created by a tangle of red tape regulations, while the organized special interests continue to pour millions of dollars through the loopholes. Small groups of concerned citizens dare not enter the political campaign fray without lawyers to guide them through the legal maze created by existing campaign reform laws. In short, laws designed to reduce the influence of special interests scare off ordinary citizens, thereby enhancing the influence of special interests.

Campaign finance laws also enhance the power of incumbents, who have access to the media by virtue of their offices and have direct access to the public through the power of press releases and junkets paid for by the taxpayers. Unfortunately, it is only incumbents who can vote on campaign finance laws—and they are obviously in favor of whatever increases their chances of keeping their jobs.

UGLINESS
IN
YOSEMITE

A visit to Yosemite National Park and its natural beauties and wonders is always an uplifting experience, even after having visited the park more than 20 years in a row. In recent years, however, the beauty of Yosemite has been tainted by the ugliness of the people who run it.

The National Park Service bureaucrats have begun systematically making it harder for people to visit Yosemite. The most blatant and arrogant example was their forcing the filling station in Yosemite Valley to close down, making the nearest source of gasoline 20 miles away.

This filling station was not spoiling some pristine wilderness. It was located near a large built-up area, which includes a sprawling hotel complex, three restaurants, a bar and a sports shop. The filling station was closed down to make it harder for people to drive their cars into Yosemite Valley.

The National Park Service bureaucrats have their own vision of how people ought to visit Yosemite and cars are not part of that vision. For years, these bureaucrats have spread hysterical and apocalyptic stories about how cars have created practically bumper-to-bumper traffic clogging the roads in the park. At no time during the dozens of visits I have made to Yosemite, during all seasons of the year, have I ever seen anything approaching the picture painted by the park's bureaucracy and spread throughout the media.

A big flood that covered Yosemite Valley to a depth of several feet in 1997 made major repairs and rebuilding necessary afterward. This rebuilding process provided an occasion and an excuse for permanently reorganizing the park, closing down camp sites and otherwise making it more difficult for people to visit Yosemite. Then, in the last months of the Clinton administration, something called The Yosemite Valley Plan was rushed through, embodying a Sierra Club type of vision of the park, sharply restricting the visits of the great unwashed in their cars, so that Sierra Club types can enjoy Yosemite in splendid isolation.

Now the taxpayers' money is being used to propagandize all visitors to the park into accepting the Yosemite Valley Plan of the park bureaucrats. Material handed out by the guards at the entrances practically gushes over how wonderful the plan is and how much more enjoyable visits will become—for those who can visit at all, under the new restrictions.

Instead of being able to drive when and where you want, under the new plan visitors will be forced to park their cars and get on buses. You can imagine families with small children, along with elderly people, all herded together and taking the regimented tour, instead of being able to stop and go when and where their own interests and need for food or toilet facilities would lead them.

It is a bureaucrats' collectivist Utopia—and anyone else's nightmare. Yet one of the bureaucrats who helped create this scheme speaks of himself as "fulfilling a sacred public trust." In fact, what he has done is the very definition of betraying a public trust—using the powers given to him to serve his own agenda, rather than what the public wants.

Like so many of the environmental storm troopers, this

official takes it upon himself to be the adjudicator between humans and animals, if not the ombudsman for the animals in Yosemite. The Yosemite Valley Plan "will benefit Yosemite's wildlife for many years to come" he says, by such things as "restoring areas in Yosemite Valley that have a high value to wildlife."

First of all, the entire Yosemite Valley is just a small fraction of Yosemite National Park. So even if it were all wall-to-wall pavement, which nobody wants, it would still barely make a dent in the amount of habitat available to animals. In this context, the park official's pious talk about reducing "habitat fragmentation" means little more than preventing those animals living in the valley from having to cross a path or a road now and then—something they do with no great sign of angst.

As a final insult to our intelligence, we are told that "generations of visitors to come" will benefit from policies that restrict visitors from coming. What the future-generations argument boils down to is this: Future generations of people with the same mindset as the environmental storm troopers will be able to impose their dictates on future generations of other people.

Arrogant ego indulgence is never pretty. But masking it as altruism makes it particularly ugly.

STATE
STEALING

A reader in Michigan says that he has been living in retirement on $15,000 a year—about $5,000 from Social Security and about $10,000 from stocks he owns in Southern California Edison. But now that the California government has forced Southern California Edison to sell electricity for less than it paid to buy it, there are no more profits from which to pay dividends, and the value of the company's stock has plummeted.

The Michigan retiree is by no means alone. All across the country there are people who have invested their savings in public utilities that supply electricity to Californians. What California politicians have done is steal these investors' money to pay for electricity that Californians want to use but are unwilling to pay for in full. Politically, it is a clever strategy to steal from people who can't vote in California, in order to gain the favor of people who can.

Long before there was any such thing as electric utility companies, governments used their power to confiscate the wealth of some and distribute it to others whose support was more important to them. The men who wrote the Constitution of the United States were well aware of that, which is why they included property rights in the Bill of Rights. For most of the history of this country, courts would not have allowed either state or federal governments to force someone to sell anything for less than it cost, because that amounts to confiscation of property without compensation.

In more recent times, unfortunately, clever people have gotten judges to evade the clear words of the Constitution by putting property rights on a lower plane than other concerns that are more politically fashionable. Law professors and others have managed to depict property rights as a special privilege of the affluent and the wealthy, something to be sacrificed on the altar of the greater good of others.

Neither these law professors nor the courts regard freedom of the press as just a special privilege of journalists. They understand that freedom of the press is an essential part of the larger political process. But they have yet to see that property rights are an essential part of the larger economic process. Without property rights, politicians have control of the whole economy within their reach, to the economic detriment of all, quite aside from the injustices they can commit against individuals.

What has allowed California politicians to get away with thefts of billions of dollars' worth of other people's property has been their ability to demonize those they are robbing and depict themselves as rescuers of Californians who are victims of "price gouging." The public's and the media's utter ignorance of economics has made this possible.

The medieval notion of a "fair and just price" seems to underlie the current notion that prices which rise above levels that people are used to are unreasonable and unconscionable. But rising costs of the fuel needed to generate electricity have to be paid for by somebody. Rising demands for electricity by people in other parts of the country compete with demands for that same electricity by Californians—and this reality underlies the rising prices that are condemned as "charging what the traffic will bear."

While utility companies that supply electricity to the public are heading into bankruptcy, the companies that supply electricity to the utilities have rising profit rates. There is nothing mysterious about this. Shortages usually cause rising prices and rising profits. These rising profits then attract the investments which end the shortage. This has been happening for centuries.

Prices are not arbitrary things. They convey a reality that is not going to be changed by price controls, whether state or federal. Prices are like readings on a thermometer. When someone is suffering from a fever, you can always lower the reading by putting the thermometer in ice water. But that does not change the reality of the fever.

The enormous costs of the current political charade in California are ultimately going to be paid for by Californians in many ways for many years ahead. Businesses disrupted by power blackouts are looking for greener pastures—or rather, states that are not so green, in the sense of environmental extremism that prevents power plants from being built. Besides, who is going to invest in building power plants in California, when existing power plants are being threatened with confiscation? Certainly not our Michigan retiree or others like him across the country.

LOVING
ENEMIES

Of all the Biblical injunctions, the one that seems hardest to keep is loving your enemies. Yet that happens with remarkable frequency in politics.

No one is a bigger enemy to women than those who promote easy sex. Many a woman has been saddled with the burden of raising a child alone, while the man responsible has gone off and forgotten all about his responsibilities. Yet feminist "leaders" have pushed easy sex and a unisex vision of the world, when in fact the consequences for women are very different—and much worse—than for men. Yet such leaders have been followed by the very women whose lives have been blighted by their philosophy.

Blacks vote overwhelmingly for liberal Democrats and yet no group has suffered more from the way liberal Democrats among politicians and judges have let violent criminals walk the streets. Moreover, no one has done more to make it illegal for the victims of these criminals to get guns to defend themselves with than liberal Democrats. No group has lost more from the dumbing down of public schools than blacks, as liberal ideas have been put into practice in the public schools.

Apparently loving your enemies isn't nearly as hard as it seems. People have been doing it throughout history.

Nobody brought more death and destruction down on

Germany than Adolf Hitler did by attacking so many countries and arousing so much of the world against his regime. By the end of World War II, many German cities were little more than vast piles of rubble, inhabited by hungry and desperate people. Yet one need only look at old newsreels of the 1930s to see the love and rapture in German crowds as they cheered their fuhrer.

At least the Germans had the excuse that they did not know in the 1930s what horrors this hate-filled demagogue would bring down on their heads in the 1940s, or what lasting disgrace would hang over Germans in general as a result of Hitler's atrocities. Even Germans whose families had lived in other countries in Europe for centuries were sent "back" to Germany by the millions, as a result of the postwar backlash against the Nazis.

On a smaller scale, we have seen charismatic cult leaders like Jim Jones in Guiana and David Koresh in Waco lead their people into lethal disasters. Jones and Koresh turned out to be the biggest enemies of their followers, though adored by them.

Dictator Juan Peron and his wife Eva were the toast of Argentina as they transformed this prosperous and vibrant country into an economic disaster area. Argentineans were as capable as anybody else of loving their enemies.

Kwame Nkrumah in Ghana, Lenin in Russia and Mao in China are among the many beloved leaders around the world who brought catastrophe to their respective peoples in this century. Napoleon was said to have been regarded as a demi-god by the troops he led to their deaths in the vast frozen reaches of Russia.

Maybe there is something in the human psyche that makes us yearn for idols. Euphoria over rock stars and mass adulation for Princess Diana are among the milder forms of this idolatry. Even so, it is painful to contrast public responses to the deaths of Mother Theresa and Princess Di within a short time of one another.

Hating your friends is apparently just as easy as loving your enemies. Ibsen wrote a play titled *An Enemy of the People* about a man who revealed dangers that others wanted to sweep under the rug, and who ended up as an outcast as a result.

The smearing of honorable men has become a highly developed political art form ever since the orchestrated demonization of Judge Robert Bork during the 1987 confirmation hearings on his nomination to the Supreme Court.

Although a similar smear campaign against Judge Clarence Thomas narrowly failed to stop his elevation to the high bench, a more all-out campaign of smears has made special prosecutor Kenneth Starr a national villain for finding out the truth about people who lied. Meanwhile, Monica Lewinsky has gotten up off her knees and gone on to collect big bucks here and overseas.

Many people find it impossible to believe the polls because these polls seem to reflect so badly on the judgment of the American public. Believe them. They are part of a long tradition.

If it turns out that we have been supporting a man who jeopardized this country's military security for the sake of political campaign contributions from China, it may be catastrophic for America someday, but it will be nothing new in history.

MICROSOFT
AND CAMPAIGN
FINANCE REFORM

When a writer from the *New York Times* was doing a story on Microsoft a few years ago, he asked their top management about the size of their lobbying office in Washington—and learned that they had no Washington office. But Microsoft's rivals in Silicon Valley have not only been lobbying, they have been contributing big bucks to the Democrats and providing Bill Clinton with an audience of cheering executives during his visits to California.

Is the Clinton Justice Department's anti-trust lawsuit against Microsoft a pay-off to those who paid political tribute and a retribution against a company that didn't? Things are seldom done that crudely or that openly in Washington. But an administration which sent dangerous technology to China, after getting illegal campaign contributions from the Chinese military, should not be assumed to be above that.

Zealots for campaign finance reform tend to see political contributions from business interests solely as bribes to get government favors. It never seems to occur to them that it could also be protection money.

Governments operating protection rackets are nothing new in history and there are gross examples around the world today. Why then is this never even considered as a possible reason for many large campaign contributions from the corporate world?

Perhaps it is nothing more than the anti-business bias of the liberal media. But whatever the reason, the campaign reform issue is shot through with hypocrisy. People who talk about the "root causes" of crime have no interest in the root causes of big bucks campaign contributions.

Whatever special political favors are gotten by this or that particular business or industry, there is no question that business as a whole is increasingly hemmed in by government regulations, mandates and pressures. In short, business as a whole has been losing its ability to mind its own business and has become increasingly a plaything for bureaucrats and politicians.

Is this what you would expect if corporate campaign contributions were just buying favors? Or is it more consistent with paying growing amounts of protection money as there have been growing numbers of government powers to be protected against?

Incidentally, Microsoft has now belatedly entered the political arena. There are even complaints that its influence is behind Congressional reluctance to appropriate the kind of money desired by the Antitrust Division of the Justice Department.

Ironically, what arouses the ire of the *New York Times* writer is that Microsoft did not have a Washington office before. That was "arrogance" on Microsoft's part, if you believe the voice of the liberal vision. When not bending the knee to politicians and not paying up for protection are considered to be "arrogance," then you know that you are in the wonderland of political punditry.

Quaint as it may be deemed these days to refer to history, the tragic fact is that many nations and many eras have been corrupted, and their economic development retarded, by precisely the kind of relationship between government and business that we have been moving toward. Put differently, American prosperity and American free enterprise are both highly unusual in the world, and we should not overlook the possibility that the two are connected.

Where those who hold political power treat businesses as prey, rather than as national assets to be safeguarded, the biggest losers are the public, whose standard of living never reaches the level of prosperity made possible by existing resources and technology.

While communism is no longer the official ideology in Russia, free enterprise has yet to be established. One painful sign of this are restrictions on the shipment of food out of particular regions controlled by political bosses, who are just as authoritarian now as they were when they were called communists.

The net result is that getting food in the cities is a problem in a country with vast expanses of some of the richest soil on the continent of Europe. The legendary fertility of the Russian black earth region caused Hitler to plan to transport trainloads of it to Germany after he conquered the country.

Whether it is rich natural resources, which abound in Russia, or high-tech know-how in which America leads the world, politicians can muck it up—to the cheers of those who think business needs throttling by government and who fear that business money will corrupt politicians.

LYING

STATISTICS

"Every year since 1950, the number of American children gunned down has doubled." Did you know that? It is just as well if you did not, because it is not true.

It takes no research to prove that it is not true. If there had been just two children in America gunned down in 1950, then doubling that number every year would have meant that, by 1980, there would have been one billion American children gunned down—more than four times the total population of the United States at that time.

Yet the claim that was quoted did not come from some supermarket tabloid. It appeared in a reputable academic journal. It is one of innumerable erroneous statistical claims generated by advocates of one cause or another. Too often, those in the media who are sympathetic to these causes repeat such claims uncritically until they become "well-known facts" by sheer repetition.

During the "homelessness" crusades of the 1980s, for example, homeless advocate Mitch Snyder made up a statistic about how many millions of homeless people there were in this country and threw it out to the media, which snapped it up and broadcast it far and wide. This fictitious number was repeated so often, and was so widely accepted, that people who actually went out and counted the homeless found that it was they who were discredited when their totals differed radically from Mitch Snyder's arbitrary number.

Only belatedly did some major media figure—Ted Koppel on "Nightline"—actually confront Mitch Snyder and ask the source of his statistic. Snyder then admitted that it was something he made up, in order to satisfy media inquiries. Moreover, homeless advocates defended what Snyder had done and called it "lying for justice."

People have been lying for centuries. What makes their statistical lies so dangerous today is that so many people in the media are ready to accept and broadcast statistics turned out by activist groups with an axe to grind—when those groups share the liberal-left orientation of the media.

Considering how many millions of dollars the TV networks pay their anchormen, surely they could spare a few bucks to hire some professional statisticians to examine the statistics that are constantly being turned out by activists, before broadcasting them as "facts." But don't hold your breath waiting for the networks to become responsible.

Hysteria sells—and accuracy takes time, which could make the news stale by the time the statisticians check it out. However, some of the claims are so ridiculous that all it would take would be to do what Ted Koppel did, ask what the data are based on.

Meanwhile, whole organizations and movements are in the business of trying to alarm the public—radical feminists, environmental extremists, race hustlers, "consumer advocates" and many more. Wild statistics help them get free publicity in the media and help stampede politicians to "do something," usually by spending the taxpayers' money to deal with a manufactured "crisis."

False statistics are only part of the problem. Even accurate statistics can be given misleading emphasis. The U.S. Bureau of the Census seems dedicated to producing statistics that emphasize differences between groups—black and white, men and women, etc.—and far less interested in statistics which indicate how much all Americans have progressed over time.

For example, in the Census' *Current Population Report* number 60-209, with voluminous statistics on all sorts of "income inequality," there is just one sentence saying that the real per capita income of whites increased by 13 percent in a decade, while that of blacks increased by 24 percent. That, apparently, is not a "politically correct" message about American society.

Perhaps the greatest distortions of statistics involve comparisons between "the rich" and "the poor"—who are mostly the same people at different stages of their lives. Most of those who were in the bottom 20 percent in 1975 were also in the top 20 percent at some point over the next 17 years. That too is not a "politically correct" message, so you seldom hear it.

The one thing that all these distortions and falsifications of statistics have in common is their thrust in the direction of creating artificial "problems" and "crises" to be dealt with by imposing government "solutions." That is apparently what makes them so attractive to the media that these shaky numbers are uncritically accepted and proclaimed to the public.

ARE WE
STILL
AMERICANS?

There was a time when Americans valued their independence and their privacy—and resented anyone who threatened either. Today, however, we put up with an incredible amount of snooping and hassles from people we could stop from bothering us if we wanted to.

Unwanted phone calls from people we don't know have now become part of the American way of life. It doesn't matter whether we are eating dinner, sleeping, sick or making love, the phone rings and interrupts us for the benefit of some stranger who wants to sell us something, solicit our money or our votes or just conduct a survey.

The simplest way to stop this would be for people to start refusing to listen to any stranger who phones them. If enough people just hang up, it will no longer pay the telemarketers to keep pestering us.

In some states, there are already laws to prevent unsolicited calls to people who have registered themselves as not wanting such calls. Why not a national law covering everybody?

It should also be against the law to sell anyone's name, address or phone number without that person's express permission. Some banks may send you some fine-print gobbledygook that most people are not going to read—and buried in all these tedious words is a notice that your personal information will be sold to others by the bank unless you specifically object. But why should the burden be on you? Where did the banks get the right to sell your privacy?

Then there are still the old-fashioned door-to-door solicitors, who want to sell, beg or get your signature for their pet crusade. Just refuse to talk to them and they too will find that it is no longer worth their while.

The electronic age has increased the number of ways that strangers can intrude on you. Some fax you their advertisements. Who gave them the right to use up other people's paper?

Perhaps the most insidious intruders are those who plant their messages in your computer, without your even being aware of it, and monitor what you are doing on the Internet. These planted items are called "cookies" for some reason. And while they are gathering information about you, you don't even know who they are or what they are up to.

You can get your computer set up to block cookies, but then the anonymous cookie monsters can bombard you with notices that another cookie is available—and that they will keep plastering this notice across your screen every time you go on the Internet, unless you accept it. One of these announcements on my computer said that they will keep showing it until the year 2009. I have to put up with this nuisance for years!

There is no point saying that we are helpless, which seems to be a big cop-out these days. Every one of us has a Congressman and two Senators. Let them know that you are sick and tired of these invasions of our privacy by people you don't even know.

No doubt the telemarketers make campaign contributions to politicians but the bottom line is that votes are what get the pols elected. If they don't get our votes, money from special interests will not save their jobs.

People who have tried to build or remodel a home discover that they are under the thumbs of a veritable army of bureaucrats, ranging from local inspectors, who can tell them what kinds of windows they can and cannot have, to the federal government which prescribes what kinds of toilets and shower heads are legal and what kinds are illegal.

When I asked a carpenter about replacing the aging deck on my house with a new one, he was horrified at the thought. A new deck would require notifying the local bureaucrats. This could then mean that, after he spent days of his time and I spent thousands of dollars, some inspector could come around and say that it had to be done all over again because of his interpretation of the local building codes. Far better to keep repairing the old deck forever.

At one time, a man's home was his castle. Today it is the bureaucrats' plaything.

Why does the public put up with this? Obviously we could vote elected officials out of office if they didn't fix the laws to get all these people off our backs. But too many of us have gotten used to being pushed around and are willing to accept it if it is washed down with pious rhetoric about safety, compassion or the environment. Why are we so ready to give up our rights for spin?

PACIFISM
AND
WAR

Although most Americans seem to understand the gravity of the situation that terrorism has put us in—and the need for some serious military response, even if that means dangers to the lives of us all—there are still those who insist on posturing, while on the edge of a volcano. In the forefront are college students who demand a "peaceful" response to an act of war. But there are others who are old enough to know better, who are still repeating the pacifist platitudes of the 1930s that contributed so much to bringing on World War II.

A former ambassador from the weak-kneed Carter administration says that we should look at the "root causes" behind the attacks on the World Trade Center and the Pentagon. We should understand the "alienation" and "sense of grievance" against us by various people in the Middle East.

It is astonishing to see the 1960s phrase "root causes" resurrected at this late date and in this context. It was precisely this kind of thinking, which sought the "root causes of crime" during that decade, creating soft policies toward criminals, which led to skyrocketing crime rates. Moreover, these soaring crime rates came right after a period when crime rates were lower than they had been in decades.

On the international scene, trying to assuage aggressors' feelings and look at the world from their point of view has had an even more catastrophic track record. A typical sample of this kind of thinking can be found in a speech to the British Parliament by Prime Minister Neville Chamberlain in 1938: "It has always seemed to me that in dealing with foreign countries we do not give ourselves a chance of success unless we try to understand their mentality, which is not always the same as our own, and it really is astonishing to contemplate how the identically same facts are regarded from two different angles."

Like our former ambassador from the Carter era, Chamberlain sought to "remove the causes of strife or war." He wanted "a general settlement of the grievances of the world without war." In other words, the British prime minister approached Hitler with the attitude of someone negotiating a labor contract, where each side gives a little and everything gets worked out in the end. What Chamberlain did not understand was that all his concessions simply led to new demands from Hitler—and contempt for him by Hitler.

What Winston Churchill understood at the time, and Chamberlain did not, was that Hitler was driven by what Churchill called "currents of hatred so intense as to sear the souls of those who swim upon them." That was also what drove the men who drove the planes into the World Trade Center.

Pacifists of the 20th century had a lot of blood on their hands for weakening the Western democracies in the face of rising belligerence and military might in aggressor nations like Nazi Germany and imperial Japan. In Britain during the 1930s, Labor Party members of Parliament voted repeatedly against military spending, while Hitler built up the most powerful military machine in Europe. Students at leading British universities signed pledges to refuse to fight in the event of war.

All of this encouraged the Nazis and the Japanese toward war against countries that they knew had greater military potential than their own. Military potential only counts when there is the will to develop it and use it, and the fortitude to continue with a bloody war when it comes. This is what they did not believe the West had. And it was Western pacifists who led them to that belief.

Then as now, pacifism was a "statement" about one's ideals that paid little attention to actual consequences. At a Labor Party rally where Britain was being urged to disarm "as an example to others," economist Roy Harrod asked one of the pacifists: "You think our example will cause Hitler and Mussolini to disarm?"

The reply was: "Oh, Roy, have you lost all your idealism?" In other words, the issue was about making a "statement"— that is, posturing on the edge of a volcano, with World War II threatening to erupt at any time. When disarmament advocate George Bernard Shaw was asked what Britons should do if the Nazis crossed the channel into Britain, the playwright replied, "Welcome them as tourists."

What a shame our schools and colleges neglect history, which could save us from continuing to repeat the idiocies of the past, which are even more dangerous now in a nuclear age.

INTENDED
CONSEQUENCES

Over the years, the phrase "unintended consequences" has come up with increasing frequency, as more and more wonderful-sounding ideas have led to disastrous results. By now, you might think that people with wonderful-sounding ideas would start to question what the consequences would turn out to be—and would devote as much time to discovering those consequences as to getting their ideas accepted and turned into laws and policies. But that seldom, if ever, happens.

Why doesn't it? Because a lot depends on what it is you are trying to accomplish. If your purpose is to achieve the heady feeling of being one of the moral elite, then that can be accomplished without the long and tedious work of following up on results.

The worldwide crusade to ban the pesticide DDT is a classic example. This crusade was begun by the much revered Rachel Carson, whose best-selling book *The Silent Spring* was based on the premise that DDT's adverse effects on the eggs of song birds would end up wiping out these species. After that, springtime would no longer be marked by birds singing; hence the silent spring.

Rachel Carson and the environmentalists she inspired have succeeded in getting DDT banned in country after country, for which they have received the accolades of many, not least their own accolades. But, in terms of the actual consequences of that crusade, there has not been a mass murderer executed in the past half-century who has been responsible for as many deaths of human beings as the sainted Rachel Carson. The banning of DDT has led to a huge resurgence of malaria in the Third World, with deaths rising into the millions.

This pioneer of the environmental movement has not been judged by such consequences, but by the inspiring goals and political success of the movement she spawned. Still less are the environmentalists held responsible for the blackouts plaguing California, despite the key role of environmental extremists in preventing power plants from being built.

The greens have likewise obstructed access to the fuels needed to generate electricity, run automobiles and trucks, and perform innumerable other tasks in the economy. Nationwide, the greens have been so successful in preventing oil refineries from being built that the last one constructed anywhere in the United States was built during the Ford administration. But environmentalists are seldom mentioned among the reasons for today's short supplies of oil and the resulting skyrocketing prices of gasoline.

Advocates of rent control are not judged by the housing shortages that invariably follow, but by their professed desire to promote "affordable housing" for all. Nor are those who have promoted price controls on food in various countries being judged by the hunger, malnutrition or even starvation that have followed. They are judged by their laudable goal of seeking to make food affordable by the poor—even if the poor end up with less food than before.

Some try to argue against the evidence for these and other counterproductive consequences of high-sounding policies.

But what is crucial is that those who advocated such policies usually never bothered to seek evidence on their own—and have resented the evidence presented by others. In short, what they advocated had the intended consequences for themselves—making them feel good—and there was far less interest in the unintended consequences for others.

Even before the rise of today's many social activist movements, T. S. Eliot understood such people and their priorities.

Writing in 1950, he said: "Half the harm that is done in this world is due to people who want to feel important. They don't mean to do harm—but the harm does not interest them. Or they do not see it, or they justify it because they are absorbed in the endless struggle to think well of themselves."

There is little hope of changing such people. But what the rest of us can do is stop gullibly accepting their ego trips as idealistic efforts for others. Above all, we need to stop letting them morally intimidate us into silence about the actual consequences of their crusades. The time is long overdue for us to insist that they put up or shut up, in terms of hard evidence about results, rather than the pious hopes that make them feel so good.

ISLAM
AND
THE WEST

Terrorist organizations in the Middle East are trying to bill the current crisis as a confrontation between Islam and the West—as in the Jihads and Crusades of centuries past. But there is no need for the rest of us to go along with that.

Six years ago, Professor Daniel Pipes of Harvard pointed out that terrorists described in the media as "Islamic fundamentalists" are often more Westernized than traditional Moslems. More recently, a leading scholar on the Middle East, Professor Bernard Lewis of Princeton, has pointed out that what these terrorists are doing—including the September 11th attack on the World Trade Center—goes counter to the teachings of Islam.

This is not a religious war, on their side or on ours. The lives of American soldiers have been risked to try to save Moslems in Somalia and the Balkans, and American aid has been poured out to help Moslem countries around the world.

What we have witnessed among today's terrorists are some of the oldest and ugliest passions of human beings in general, based on envy and resentment, rather than on any religious teachings. Some fatuous people on college campuses, and in other enclaves of the intelligentsia and the glitterati, have tried to suggest that we must have done something to cause terrorists to attack us. What we have done is have achievements that dwarf theirs.

A thousand years ago, it was the other way around. The Islamic world at that time was far more advanced than the West. It was not only militarily stronger, but also more advanced in science, mathematics, and scholarship.

Contrary to the dogmas of the egalitarians, some portion of the human race has always been far in advance of others. In earlier centuries it was China and in later centuries it was Europe and America. The only egalitarian principle is that no one has been permanently superior.

As the human race has evolved over the millennia, some peoples have taken the lead during one era and others during other eras. Sometimes the reasons seem clear but at other times no one really knows why. The vast majority of people in all cultures are too busy with their own personal cares and concerns to give much thought to such things. Unfortunately, the rising prosperity of the world in general has supported the rise of increasing numbers of people who have the luxury of becoming preoccupied—or even obsessed—with such imponderables.

It is not poverty, but time on their hands to brood, that has produced all sorts of fanaticisms. Many of the leaders of these fanaticisms have come from wealthy families, like Osama bin Laden today and like Karl Marx and Friedrich Engels in the 19th century. The poor can seldom spare the time or resources for such things.

What have Americans done to arouse such people? We have succeeded. No, our foreign policies have not always been flawless or even always consistent—but neither have anyone else's. Still, it is not what we have done wrong that provokes their wrath. It is what we have done right, leading us to surpass them.

Nothing is easier than to blame those who lead for the problems of those who lag. "Exploitation" theories have flourished around the world, in defiance of mountains of evidence, because they say that the rich are rich because the poor are poor. It is a psychological coup, even when it is economic nonsense.

Too many Americans fall for such ideological visions. Not most, but too many. Even in the wake of the terrible catastrophe of September 11th, and with the prospect of still more such lethal attacks looming ahead, they cannot resist an opportunity to try to be morally one-up on their fellow Americans by suggesting that our misbehavior must have provoked these attacks. They simply cannot bring themselves to confront the reality of deliberate evil.

Two World Wars were launched in the 20th century by countries seeking to find "a place in the sun"—that is, for ego. Rationalistic excuses cannot hide that brutal reality.

Two centuries ago, Edmund Burke said: "There is no safety for honest men except by believing all possible evil of evil men." If we haven't learned that lesson now, what will it take for us to learn it?

Incidentally, has anyone considered that, if pilots had not been forbidden to carry guns, there might be thousands of Americans still alive today and the World Trade Center still standing?

PANDERING
TO THE
ANOINTED

In politically correct California, there are two things you must believe in, if you want to be regarded as a decent human being—"open spaces" and "affordable housing." The fact that these two things contradict each other is of interest only to those who are old-fashioned enough to take logic and evidence seriously.

Economists may talk about how supply and demand determine prices. But, in California, there is not the slightest discussion of the very possibility that reducing the supply of land by taking it off the market drives up the price of the remaining land and the housing built on it.

Here, on the left coast, high prices are considered inexplicable or explicable only by "greed" on the part of landlords. Presumably, other landlords in other places are just nicer people.

One of the reasons housing is not affordable in many parts of California is that there are so many people devoted to keeping it from being built. An absolutely stereotypical specimen of this mind-set is a middle-aged hippie and Berkeley dropout who has devoted himself to "saving" something called "San Bruno Mountain."

Only if you call a hill 1,300 feet high a mountain does even the word make sense. Moreover this is not some rural Walden.

It is a hill next to the baseball park where the San Francisco Giants played for years.

Like other things, this hill can be used for many different purposes. When other people use it for what they want, that is called "destroying" San Bruno. When the Berkeley hippies of the world use it for what they want to, that is called "saving" it.

Now that we know the local language, we can understand why the *San Francisco Chronicle* lavishes praises on the San Bruno activist "in his black plastic sandals" for saving "his beloved San Bruno Mountain." Of course, if this really was his mountain—or even hill—there would be no story. What someone does with his own property is of little interest or concern to anyone else.

The reason there is a story is that this hill does not belong to the hippie activist at all. He simply arrogates to himself the right to obstruct other people from building on it, whether by chaining himself to a construction fence, organizing other activists or propagandizing school children who are brought there by their teachers to learn political correctness from a local guru, instead of spending their time on anything so mundane as reading, writing and arithmetic.

Meanwhile, a few miles to the west, there are nearly 1,500 acres of rolling land that San Francisco has acquired from the federal government after a military base was closed there. That is nearly twice the size of Central Park. Surely this could add a vast amount of housing to the city's supply and ease the strains that have everyone wringing his hands over a lack of affordable housing.

Not on your life. No way is this vast stretch of real estate to be allowed to fall into the grubby hands of developers, who would build housing for the unwashed masses. It too has to be preserved for the benefit of the nobler sorts.

One set of these precious people favored by the political powers that be call themselves the San Francisco Film Centre. Note that it is not movies but "film" and that the American way of spelling "center" is not good enough for them.

How did they get onto this land? The *San Francisco Chronicle* explains: "A seven-member panel of business, community and government leaders, appointed by the Clinton administration, reviews proposals from prospective tenants and decides who gets to occupy the converted historic buildings."

In other words, the old collectivist way of doing things, which has failed repeatedly on every inhabited continent and among people of every race and creed, is to be used to dispose of this land. The operation is supposed to "achieve financial self-sufficiency by 2013."

Can you imagine an area twice the size of Central Park taking more than a decade to get out of the red, in a city dying for more housing? Not if it were put on the market and the buyers were free to construct apartment buildings.

If this were just the usual story of political favoritism and corruption, that would be one thing. But this is the deeper corruption of people whose self-indulgence and ego trips are portrayed as some kind of noble concern for higher things.

GREEN BIGOTS
VERSUS
HUMAN BEINGS

The red-legged frog is only the latest of many supposedly endangered species whose habitats may be kept off-limits to human beings, even if that means stopping the building of much-needed housing. We have grown so used to having the interests of millions of human beings sacrificed for some allegedly endangered species that we no longer stop and think about how outrageous that is.

Too often we even buy the notion that the shrill and self-righteous people who push this stuff are some kind of noble crusaders, thinking only of the higher things, instead of as the selfish and arrogant bigots and bullies that they are.

The essence of bigotry is claiming for yourself rights that you would deny to others. The green bigots who call themselves environmentalists do this all the time. They also lie a lot, as self-anointed idealists often do.

Some species that have been said to be endangered have turned out to be very abundant and other creatures that may in fact be endangered are not species. Frogs are a species, but every conceivable variant of a frog is not a species.

How many people have ever seen a red-legged frog? Or even want to see a red-legged frog? The green bigots may be horrified that there are people who don't have the slightest interest in red-legged frogs. But those people are just as much

American citizens as any life-long member of the Sierra Club and are entitled to equal rights under the Constitution. There is neither a legal nor a moral reason to over-ride what they want because the green bigots want something else.

Like others who seek special privileges, the green bigots claim to be speaking for others—"future generations," for example. But this is just shifting the argument to a different venue, without changing it in the slightest. Those people who don't give a darn about red-legged frogs are going to have future descendants, just as much as the environmental extremists will. What the green bigots really want is for future generations of green bigots to be able to over-ride future generations of other people who do not share their views.

Fuzzy words and apocalyptic visions are stock in trade for the green bigots, who are forever referring to "fragile" environments—but with no definition of "fragile," much less any evidence to fit a definition. I should be so "fragile" that I could survive thousands of years of earthquakes, forest fires and mountainous glaciers rolling over me.

What some consider to be idealism could more accurately be called self-exaltation. What could be more exalting than to take on the God-like role of adjudicating between animals and people? You cannot be a judge handing down edicts for others unless you are placing yourself above those others. We know how judges are appointed or elected. But who elected the green bigots to play God?

Election is the last thing they have in mind. Instead, they infiltrate coastal commissions, zoning boards and other federal, state and local bureaucracies, from which they can impose their edicts on others, without being accountable for the consequences. A large part of the blame for California's electricity crisis is due to green bigots who have conducted a scorched earth policy against anyone trying to build power-generating plants there.

A new cult of pagan nature worship has sprung up, in which the slightest inconvenience to any toad or bug is enough to call a halt to even the most urgent human needs. A new mythology has been created, in which wildlife can only survive in their original habits. Spotted owls supposedly can live only in "old growth" forests, though there must have been a time when the old growth trees were new growth trees. Surely they have not been there since the dawn of time or even throughout the whole history of spotted owls.

When you see birds nesting in metropolitan skyscrapers, you have to acknowledge that wild creatures do have some adaptability—unless you think these are "old growth" sky-scrapers. Species could not have survived the evolutionary changes of the earth if they didn't have some adaptability. But now, everything is to be frozen where it is by the green big-ots—and at unlimited costs to others.

Nature worship is fine for those who want it. I have nothing against faith-based organizations. But a theocracy impos-ing its will on others is something else, even when it is a theocracy of nature-worshippers.

ANOTHER
OUTRAGE

Nothing is an outrage when the reigning fad is being non-judgmental. So perhaps it is not surprising that there has been no nationwide chorus of condemnation of Bill Clinton's anti-American speech at Georgetown University. According to the former president, America is "paying a price today" for slavery in the past and for the fact that "native Americans were dispossessed and killed."

Can you name a country, anywhere in the world, where there has never been slavery? Can you name a country, anywhere in the world, where land has not changed hands as a result of military conquest?

It is a painful commentary on human beings that there are no such countries. But it is hogwash to single out the United States for sins that have afflicted the entire human race.

And to say that Americans are paying a price today because of those sins is grotesque. Nobody in the World Trade Center owned any slaves or killed any Indians. This pushing of collective guilt, inherited from centuries past, is a shameless hustle that insults our intelligence.

All around the world, there are cities that have had different names at different periods of history because they were conquered again and again by different invaders. Istanbul was

Constantinople before it was conquered, Bratislava was Pressburg, New York was New Amsterdam—and so on and on.

Just for the record, slavery was abolished throughout Western civilization more than a century before it was abolished in the Islamic world—for it is not completely abolished in the Islamic world to this very moment. But double standards are at the heart of the hustle. Nobody else is going to cough up the money that the hustlers want from the United States.

Clinton wants us to pay for the education of children in other countries because it is "a lot cheaper than going to war." This kind of talk is considered Deep Stuff by shallow people.

According to Clinton, Americans "have to get rid of our arrogant self-righteousness so that we don't claim for ourselves things we deny to others." If other people don't have what we have, does that mean that we denied it to them?

Are people around the world to be encouraged to look to us as their sugar daddy, instead of looking to themselves to do the things that have lifted other countries from poverty to prosperity? The whole world was once poorer than today's Third World and there was nobody to give them foreign aid.

We should also forgive Third World debt, according to Clinton.

What this means, in plain English, is that American taxpayers should be lied to when they are told that their money is being lent overseas, because no one should expect the loans to be repaid. It also means that no one should expect adult responsibility from Third World rulers, who live lavishly, build monuments to themselves and stash money in Swiss bank accounts.

The vast sums of money that can be borrowed legitimately from private lenders in international financial markets make it wholly unnecessary for Third World governments to "borrow" from the U.S. government in the first place. The difference is that private borrowing requires adult responsibility and investing the money in something that is going to actually produce some tangible benefits for people other than rulers and bureaucrats.

Not content with playing the slavery card and the conquest card, Clinton went back centuries before there was a United States to regale the Georgetown students with the atrocities of the Crusaders against the Moslems, saying "we are still paying for it." Were there no atrocities the other way? Or among people on every inhabited continent, for centuries on end? But again, there is a double standard, of which the Blame America First ideology is just one example.

Bill Clinton closed by saying that the issue revolves around "the nature of truth." Who would have thought that he was an expert on truth? Incidentally, as has often happened, he arrived 45 minutes late, keeping a thousand people waiting. But that was only the beginning of his irresponsibility.

THE BEST
OF THE
CENTURY

Who was the best leader of the 20th century? My nomination goes to Winston Churchill. If one man ever pulled a whole nation through a crisis which threatened its very existence, that man was Churchill, prime minister of Britain during the dark days of the Nazi blitz in 1940, when London was bombed night after night and a German invasion force was assembled on the other side of the English Channel. Most people did not expect Britain to survive.

It is hard to convey to a new generation today how close Britain came to annihilation and how close Hitler came to becoming master of the whole continent of Europe. Imagine now this monster, with all the immense resources of the continent at his disposal and in control of the huge British navy, while his Japanese allies were in control of the richest natural resources in the conquered countries of Southeast Asia.

How long would the position of the United States have been tenable, with no allies and with the most formidable military forces ever assembled arrayed against us? By now, Americans might be speaking German—except for those of us who would not be speaking at all, because we would have gone up in smoke in Hitler's extermination camps.

This was more than just another war. The Nazi ideology was, as *Time* magazine put it, "a revolution against the human soul," conceived by Hitler "in conscious contempt for the life, dignity and freedom of individual man." Nothing that we could call civilization would have survived the triumph of this barbaric creed, armed with the weapons of modern science.

After an unbroken string of devastating military triumphs—over-running France in a matter of weeks and other countries in a matter of days—the Nazis were finally stopped only by the British refusal to surrender in the face of overwhelming odds.

That was what Churchill will be remembered for. Unlike the French, who declared Paris an open city, rather than see its historic treasures bombed, Churchill said, "It is better that London should lie in ruins and ashes than that we should surrender."

The inspiration of this great man not only saved Britain, the disruption of the Nazi timetable for conquest bought time for a woefully unprepared United States to finally begin building up its military defenses. It is enough of a claim to historic greatness for a man to have saved his own country. Churchill may have saved civilization.

After the Nazis and their Japanese allies were finally vanquished, there remained the long and unprecedentedly dangerous Cold War with the Communists internationally. Moreover, within Western democracies themselves, the welfare state and socialism—beautiful in theory and poisonous in practice—were stifling growth and producing double-digit inflation and double-digit unemployment at the same time, with accompanying social degeneration and demoralization.

Two leaders turned this around—Prime Minister Margaret Thatcher in Britain and President of the United States Ronald Reagan. They triumphed both domestically and internationally over forces that many thought could not be defeated even singly, much less together.

Who would have dreamed that socialist Britain would begin selling whole government-run industries back to private enterprise?

Who would have thought that the death grip of the British labor unions on the economy could be broken?

Ronald Reagan not only turned around the decline of the American economy, he defied the conventional wisdom by basing his foreign policy on a military buildup, designed to force the Soviet Union to change its foreign policy and end the arms race. Reagan even predicted that we were seeing the last days of this evil empire.

Few believed him and many scoffed. But he succeeded where a whole succession of other presidents had failed.

These were clearly the three greatest leaders of this century. It is painful to imagine what the world would be like today without them.

PART IV
EDUCATIONAL ISSUES

THE
WRONG
FILTER

Headlines were made by the results of the Third International Mathematics and Science Study. Yet nobody should have been surprised, since our students have been doing badly on international tests for decades.

American 12th graders fell below the international average in general mathematics and general science. In advanced mathematics, our students were tied for last place and in physics they had sole possession of last place.

Students from Asian nations, who usually do very well on such tests, did not take part in these particular tests. So American students are trailing the pack among the also-rans.

While the American educational system is falling behind academically, it is leading the world in excuses. One of these excuses is that more of our students reach the 12th grade, so that we are comparing our average with other countries' elites.

While that may be true for some countries, there are other countries that have as high a percentage of their students finish secondary school as we do—and some have a higher percentage completing secondary education. Both kinds of countries beat out our students.

Another excuse is that our population has so many disadvantaged minorities that this drags down the average. But when you compare our very top students with the top students from other countries, ours still get clobbered.

U.S. Secretary of Education Richard Riley responded to the sad results from these international tests by calling them "unacceptable." Nonsense! Such dismal results have been accepted for years and will be accepted for years to come, so long as the National Education Association continues to contribute millions of dollars to political campaigns.

From the standpoint of the NEA, the American public schools are not a failure but a great big success. These schools provide NEA members with jobs where they have iron-clad tenure, automatic raises, and no accountability for bad performances by their students or themselves.

The public schools also have a virtual monopoly on the supply of schoolchildren, except for those whose parents are affluent enough to be able to afford private schools or dedicated enough to homeschool their children. What this all adds up to is that the public schools can do pretty much whatever they want to, including avoiding academic training and indulging themselves in all sorts of fads and psychobabble, including "self-esteem."

In this latest round of international tests, American students led the world in one department: "self-esteem." As in previous international tests, American students had the highest perception of how well they had done. Seventy percent said that they thought they had done well. This would be comic if it were not so tragic.

While there are many particular things that can be criticized in our public schools, even the critics often miss the point when they fail to see that the key to all these counter-productive policies are the people who make them. If we purged the public schools of all the time-wasting silliness there today, we would have accomplished little if the same kinds of people were left in place to bring in new non-academic nonsense tomorrow.

Innumerable tests over many decades have shown that the mental test scores of people who specialize in education are among the lowest of any college students. This is not an accident. Given the incredibly bad courses in education that abound, in even the top universities, intelligent people are repelled, while mediocrities and incompetents sail through.

If you are not going to change that, then you are not going to change the low quality of American public schools. Education courses are a filter. They filter out intelligent students and let mediocrities pass through.

Just as you are not going to catch ocean fish in mountain lakes, no matter how expensive your fishing equipment, so you are not going to get an academically proficient or even academically oriented class of people coming out of education schools and education courses. First-rate people do not come out of such places because they do not go into such places or do not stay if they do.

Raising teachers' salaries will not do it. You will just get more expensive mediocrities in the classroom and more expensive incompetents being graduated from our schools.

TOO MANY Ph.D.s?

When anyone who owns a business discovers that unsold products are piling up on the shelf or in the warehouse, it doesn't take a rocket scientist to figure out that it is time to cut back production until the inventory declines. But no such logic applies in the academic world.

Complaints about the excess number of Ph.D.s in the humanities have gone on for years. The answer? Have the government create new programs to hire the excess Ph.D.s that no one else wants to hire. Create more post-doctoral fellowships, so that the taxpayers can carry these people for a few more years before they are finally forced out into the cruel world that the rest of us live in all the time.

Every year, for 12 consecutive years, American universities have broken all previous records for the number of Ph.D.s awarded. The number of doctorates awarded in 1997 was nearly one-third larger than it was just a decade earlier. Forget about supply and demand when it comes to academia.

Ironically, doctorates in science, engineering and mathematics have come down somewhat in recent years, even though American companies are recruiting engineers from India, Russia and other places. But in English, history and other humanities fields, the graduate schools are flooding the market with people for whom there are no jobs.

Behind all these strange goings-on in academia is the simple fact that colleges and universities are spending other people's money—and neither the donors nor the taxpayers have the time to monitor what is happening on campuses across the country.

Professors of English gain prestige and professional advancement by spinning esoteric theories of literature and promoting other avant-garde notions. Whether the sophomores understand English grammar or know any adjectives beyond "awesome" is not their problem. Lower-level courses are taught disproportionately by graduate students who are working toward their own Ph.D.s and earning a meager salary by teaching basic courses that professors disdain to teach.

Reduce the number of graduate students and professors will be forced to sully their hands teaching introductory courses, instead of spending their time preparing papers on sexuality and Sophocles for the Modern Language Association meetings. It is impossible to caricature the papers presented at the Modern Language Association meetings. Indeed, it is impossible to cite some of the titles in a family newspaper.

A rich country like the United States can afford to waste money on many foolish projects. But no country can afford the degeneration and internal strife bred by idle hands for whom the devil finds work.

Among the great curses of the Third World are large numbers of people with degrees and the pretensions that go with them, but without any productive skills to contribute to raising the material standard of living in those countries. Worse, these superfluous degree-holders promote political instability and economic chaos through demagoguery and policies based on fashionable ideologies that have never had to stand the test of results.

It has taken decades for Latin America to get over "dependency theory" that blamed that region's lag behind the industrial nations of Europe and North America on the evil machinations of Yankees and other imperialists. The living standards of whole generations have been sacrificed trying out policies based on half-baked theories that each country should become "independent" of the world market by producing its own products to substitute for the products it formerly imported.

Nor has Latin America been alone in promoting self-defeating economic policies, based on the ideological fashions of superfluous degree-holders. It took many African countries decades of disastrous experiments with socialistic policies before some of them belatedly turned away from these nostrums and toward market-oriented policies that have finally begun raising their people's standards of living above where they were when they were colonies of European imperialist powers.

The United States is not a Third World country, of course. But it has many less fortunate people, whose aspirations for a better life can be needlessly frittered away by ideas from those who have been shielded from reality in the name of education.

"NO
EXCUSES"

Tests show that most low-income students in the 8th grade still cannot multiply or divide two-digit numbers by other two-digit numbers. That is, they cannot tell you what 14 times 15 equals or what 60 divided by 12 is.

Against this background, you might think that there would be enormous interest in those particular low-income and minority schools where the students equal or exceed the national norms in verbal or mathematical skills. But you would be wrong.

Some of these successful schools have had to run a gauntlet of hassles from education bureaucrats. A principal of a successful minority school in California was hassled because she used phonics instead of "whole language" and because she taught foreign-born children in English instead of the various languages in the bilingual programs. The fact that she was succeeding where others were failing did not exempt her from being harassed.

In Massachusetts, a principal had trouble even getting approval to set up a school that would be using standardized tests to assess the progress of his students, most of whom were from minority groups. He was called a "racist" and a "Nazi." His students ended up with the highest test scores in town. Some Nazi!

However phony the accusation, the hostility behind it was very real. The education establishment—the teachers' unions, the schools of education, and state and federal education bureaucrats—are out to protect their turf and their dogmas at all costs. People who challenge their beliefs, in words or deeds, are to be denounced, demonized, harassed or otherwise driven from the scene.

Despite having to buck the education establishment, some brave principals and teachers have created oases of excellence for low-income, minority students in a vast educational desert. A recently published book titled *No Excuses* by Samuel Casey Carter provides sketches of 21 such schools, scattered around the country.

Again and again, this book shows schools where minority students from the bottom of the socioeconomic scale are scoring above the national average on standardized tests that are supposed to be so "culturally biased" that only white, middle-class students can do well on them. That is one of the many widely-used excuses by "educators" who fail to educate. And that is why the very different philosophy in these successful schools is called a "No Excuses" philosophy—no excuses for students or teachers.

How have successful schools for low-income, minority students done it? Largely by ignoring education "experts" and going against the theories and practices that reign elsewhere in American schools. Those schools which have low-income black, Hispanic and other minority students scoring higher than many white, middle-class students elsewhere in math and English typically feature real teaching rather than "activities" or "projects," phonics rather than "whole language," standardized tests rather than mushy evaluations, and in general a back-to-basics approach.

However, do not think for one moment that the fact that

one theory of education fails and another succeeds is going to change the people who run our public schools or who control our teachers' colleges. Those people have tenure and their pay is not affected in the slightest by whether or not they produce educated students.

Even incompetent teachers are hard to get rid of in most public school systems. In New York state, it takes an average of 15 months and more than $170,000 to fire one teacher.

From the standpoint of the education establishment in general, and the teachers' unions in particular, our education system is not a failure, even though American children usually finish at or near the bottom in international tests. The public school system is a success for those who run it, in terms of protecting their jobs, their turf, their dogmas and—above all—their power to use vulnerable children as guinea pigs for the fads that come and go.

Parents, voters and taxpayers also need to understand that our public schools are not failing. They are succeeding in substituting self-serving agendas for the task of conveying the accumulated knowledge of the past to today's younger generation.

While there are many serious social problems making it harder to educate children today, there are nevertheless schools which succeed in spite of those problems—but only because education is their top priority.

Get a copy of *No Excuses*. It is published by the Heritage Foundation in Washington.

BACK
DOOR
QUOTAS

Ever since racial quotas in college admissions were banned by Proposition 209 in California and by the 5th Circuit Court of Appeals in Texas, academics and politicians have been racking their brains to come up with something that would allow quotas to continue under new names.

The latest attempt to get away from admitting students by their own individual qualifications is a proposal from the president of the University of California that the standard Scholastic Aptitude Test (SAT I) no longer be required of students applying for college admissions.

According to UC President Richard C. Atkinson, an "overemphasis on the SAT is distorting educational priorities and practice." Moreover, "the test is perceived by many as unfair" and its results "can have devastating impact on the self-esteem and aspirations of young students."

This is a masterpiece of mushiness. How much emphasis is "over" emphasis? And if that is really the problem, then why not simply reduce the emphasis instead of throwing out the test? But of course this was just a talking point, so it would be unfair to expect either evidence or logic to back up the claim of "over" emphasis, much less a rational response in the unlikely event that this could be demonstrated.

As for the test being "perceived" as unfair, what isn't? And how many other people perceive it as fairer than the alternatives? Arbitrarily singling out those who have one opinion as the one to follow would allow anybody to advocate any policy (or its opposite) on any issue, anywhere and any time.

The same goes for the "self-esteem" argument. Believe me, my self-esteem would suffer if I had to go out on a golf course and compete with Tiger Woods or onto a tennis court and compete with Pete Sampras or Andre Agassi. We would have to throw out every criterion in every field if we wanted to avoid damaging the self-esteem of those who fail.

But do not think that a madman is in charge of the University of California. Dr. Atkinson must know better. These are standard arguments by those who want to bring quotas in by the back door, when they can no longer come in the front door.

These ploys are not even confined to the United States. When courts in India put limits on how far group quotas could go, all sorts of non-academic factors suddenly blossomed in the university admissions process. Subjective factors like "aptitude" and "general abilities" were given great weight, even when these were assessed in interviews that lasted only three minutes per applicant. Dr. Atkinson seeks similar "holistic" criteria.

In India, subjective factors were clearly being used as automatic offsets to differences in academic qualifications. As one Indian court put it, there was a "disturbing" pattern of discrepancy between interview rankings and rankings on other criteria. Students with unsatisfactory academic records nevertheless received "very high marks at the interviews," while "a large number of students who had secured very high marks in the university examinations and who performed well in their earlier class had secured low marks at the interviews."

In short, inconvenient academic criteria were being gotten

rid of, so that group quotas could continue in new disguises. That is precisely what getting rid of standardized academic tests is all about. Similarly, admitting the top X percent of each high school's graduates is more of the same deceptive sleight-of-hand. The top 10 percent of students from one high school may be less qualified than the merely average student from another high school.

The claim is often made that the SAT is "culturally biased." But life itself is culturally biased. If you can't handle math and the English language, you are in big trouble.

If the "culturally biased" argument is meant to insinuate that these tests falsely predict a lower academic achievement level for minority students than they later achieve, then that is a purely factual question. And the facts have devastated that theory time and again, for years on end. No wonder the quota crowd don't want to define exactly what they mean by "culturally biased," nor put it to the test of facts.

The tests are not unfair. Life is unfair. If you are serious about wanting minority students to have a better chance in life, then you need to start years before they take the SAT. And you need to stop deceiving them and the American people.

WE ARE
ALL
"DROPOUTS"

Hats off to Jackson Toby, who wrote in *The Weekly Standard* what few have dared to say in the past three decades: "Let them drop out." He argues that too many students are finding nothing but frustration and resentment at being trapped for hours every day in high schools that are boring and meaningless to them.

This argument was made back in the 1960s by the late and great Edward Banfield in his classic book, *The Unheavenly City*. Moreover, he had hard facts to back up what he said. Studies indicated that it was not dropping out that led youngsters into delinquency and crime but staying in school after they had lost all interest in it and lost all respect for it.

Nevertheless, incessant propaganda from the education establishment has made the word "dropout" one that inspires horror. But all of us are dropouts—and should be. At some point or other, we all leave the educational system.

Some leave in high school, some leave after high school, some leave in or after college and others leave after completing a Ph.D. or after finishing a post-doctoral fellowship. But nobody's whole life is spent going to school. Nor should it be.

The right point at which to leave varies enormously from person to person. So does the time to come back, as millions do.

This is ultimately a very individual decision, if we are thinking about either the wellbeing of the students or the wellbeing of society. But if we are thinking about children in school as meal tickets for the education establishment—which is often paid on the basis of "average daily attendance"—then the way to maximize that money is to hold as many kids hostage as long as possible and demonize the word "dropout."

When mere rhetoric and repetition are not enough, the education establishment points to the fact that high school graduates earn more money than dropouts, and college graduates earn still more. But one of the first things you learn in Statistics 1 is that correlation is not causation. Unfortunately, it is also one of the first things that many people forget.

The youngsters who drop out of high school are different from those who graduate. Keeping everybody in high school to the bitter end will not change this difference in people, just as joining a basketball team will not make you any taller, even though statistics show that basketball players are usually taller than other people.

Most people who drop out of high school resume their education at some later point, either to complete high school or learn a trade or get admitted to college without a high school diploma (like yours truly). These individuals and their incomes are not counted in statistics about the earnings of high school dropouts.

Given the incredible amounts of time that are wasted on non-academic "activities" and "projects" in most public schools, the 12 years it currently takes to complete high school could easily be reduced to 8 years, if not 6, just by getting the junk out of the curriculum and doing some serious teaching of math, English and other basic skills.

This would lessen the burden and the boredom, enabling

many more youngsters to complete their elementary and secondary education. It would also rid the school of the negative and disruptive influence of those students who have no interest in what the school is doing. It would also reduce the pressures to dumb down everyone's education, in hopes of getting the disinterested to stay on for the sake of appearances and fun activities.

It would also shorten the time that youngsters spend in an adolescent subculture and begin sooner the process of their joining the adult world, where they can learn from people who have a lot more experience and maturity than they or their peers have. It might be possible to debate all these various considerations from the standpoint of what is best for the individual and the society. But none of that really matters to the educational establishment.

Their jobs depend on having a large captive audience, and the self-interest of "educators" is served by extending the period of students' incarceration—starting earlier in kindergarten and preschool, and including summer school for all. There will never be a lack of high-sounding excuses for these exercises in promoting the self-interest of teachers unions and educational bureaucrats.

Only if more parents and voters start looking beyond the rhetoric and spin is the present bad situation likely to change. But have their own years of dumbed-down education made that unlikely?

SCHOOL
TO
SCHOOL?

One of the problems of getting old is that you miss out on so many of the exciting new things that young people enjoy. Often this is because what is new to them is something that has been tried again and again in the past—and has turned out to be a bummer again and again.

One of the many idiotic ideas that reappears in our public schools in new verbal guises is the idea that the school should be preparing young people for the world of work. Since every old idea has to have a new name, this is now called the "school-to-work" program, sponsored by the federal government and spending billions of tax dollars.

This used to be called "vocational guidance" and the idea goes back at least 90 years, when the gurus of so-called progressive education said that schools spent too much time on academic subjects and not enough time on "practical" things that would be "relevant" to the kind of work and life that students would go into after finishing school.

In the latest reincarnation of vocational guidance as school-to-work programs, 8th graders are given tests to determine what kinds of jobs they are supposedly suited for and they are asked to make career choices. Such choices are premature by at least a decade. Some of the best liberal arts colleges allow—and encourage—their students to take two years of general education in college before deciding what subject to major in.

Such choices are too serious to make without some solid basis. You may be fascinated by chemistry experiments in high school, but that is very different from saying that you can master the difficult analytical skills required for majoring in chemistry in college. Every college has students who enroll in pre-med programs and end up majoring in sociology.

What did you really know about careers when you were in the 8th grade? I didn't even know what an economist was and had never heard of a think tank, such as the Hoover Institution, where I have worked for 20 years. Nor is it at all realistic to expect school teachers to have any such encyclopedic knowledge of the thousands of occupations out there today, much less what the trends are for various fields in the years ahead, when these 8th graders will be working adults.

When meteorologists have trouble predicting the weather five days ahead and financial experts can get clobbered in the stock market, what in the world would lead anybody to seriously expect school teachers to predict the world in which their 8th graders will be living, decades from now? The high rates of obsolescence of jobs and skills doom any such efforts.

In an age when "educators" seem to be constantly trying to find things to do instead of educating, school-to-work is just another of those irresponsible self-indulgences which create the illusion that they are doing something useful, when in fact they are wasting precious time and spreading confusion among the young.

It is worse than that. School-to-work programs are also indoctrination programs for politically correct views about careers. They test for attitudes as well as aptitudes. Once you start playing little tin god, micro-managing other people's lives, it is hard to know where to stop. In reality, the place to stop is before you begin.

School is not a place for make-believe practicality. Schools need to do what they have a special advantage and a special time for doing—conveying to the young the basic skills that they are going to need, irrespective of the particular jobs they may have, which no one can predict anyway.

More important, people need to be educated as citizens and as human beings. For that, they need to be able to draw upon the wisdom of the ages—whether expressed in mathematics, science, history or literature not the fads of the moment.

Employers are not demanding that job applicants show up knowing all about the work on the first day. But they need people who can read well enough to understand written instructions—and many employers complain that the schools are not supplying that.

Some employers are hiring engineers from India and Russia, not because they are better engineers, but because they have been taught the English language better than many Americans.

What we really need is a school-to-school program, not programs in which schools pretend to be what they cannot possibly be.

THE WAR
AGAINST
BOYS

The old saying, "Boys will be boys," has long since become obsolete in schools across the length and breadth of this country. Unknown to most parents, there are federally-financed programs to prevent boys from acting the way boys have always acted before.

The things done by those who have taken on the role of changing boys range from forbidding them from running and jumping during recess to having them wear dresses and pretend to be girls or women in the classroom.

Whatever the particular mix of things done at a particular school, it is accompanied by a barrage of propaganda prepared by radical feminists for nationwide distribution with the blessing—and the money—of the U.S. Department of Education.

The people who are doing this see their role as changing your children into the kinds of people they want them to be—not the kind of people you want them to be. Parents who somehow learn what is going on in school and object are told that "studies prove" that this is the right thing to do, that "specialists" and "experts" know more about this than parents can possibly know.

A newly published book titled *The War Against Boys* by Christina Hoff Sommers not only reveals what these brainwashing programs are doing, it also shows that the so-called "studies" on which these programs are based are either hope-lessly inadequate or just plain non-existent. Christina Hoff Sommers is a scholar at the American Enterprise Institute and she not only sees through the fraudulent claims of the radical feminists, she is familiar with real studies—both here and overseas—which show the direct opposite of what the brain-washers claim.

The people who are promoting the anti-male agenda are experts at nothing except manipulating the media and snow-ing gullible educators, who are more interested in puffing themselves up as "agents of social change" than in teaching children. Boys in elementary school, or even kindergarten, have been punished for being politically incorrect toward girls.

One nine-year-old boy who reached for a piece of fruit in a school lunch line and accidentally brushed against a girl was arrested, hand-cuffed and fingerprinted for sexual harass-ment, even though the charges later had to be dropped. A boy of three was punished in school for hugging another child. The feminist dogma is that such things are precursors of wife-beating, rape and other crimes of men against women—and so must be nipped in the bud.

According to these propagandists, 4 million American women are beaten to death by men every year. That is four times as many American women as die from all causes put together. The actual number of women killed by men is less than one percent of what was claimed.

However inaccurate and irresponsible the propaganda, it is very effective in creating the kind of paranoia that gets brainwashing programs and draconian punishment of boys into the schools. Staggering as it is to realize that schools are using materials and creating rules based on sheer dogma and outright lies, the tragic fact is that such tactics have been common in totalitarian countries throughout this century. What is uncommon is their pervasiveness in America over the past generation.

Radical feminists apply the old Hitler-Goebbels doctrine that the people will believe any lie, if it is big enough and told often enough and loud enough. Intimidation and retribution against all who dare to disagree is likewise as much a part of the new agenda as it was in the old totalitarian regimes.

The War Against Boys shows where the propagandists have gotten their facts wrong—where they have any facts at all. But the brainwashers' goals are not accuracy but power. In those terms, they have been an incredible success. They are no more interested in facts than any other power-seekers. Did Hitler study genetics?

Christina Hoff Sommers writes not only as a scholar but as the mother of two boys. Her book is must-reading, not only for parents of boys in school, but for all parents, and should inform any responsible citizen and voter who is concerned about American education.

Tragically, radical feminists are just one of many reckless zealots who have turned our schools into ideological indoctrination centers, instead of places for children to get an education in basic skills. One of the reasons American children do so badly in international tests of academic skills is that our schools are preoccupied with politically correct social crusades.

"RESEARCH"
MARCHES
ON

If you have tears, prepare to shed them. *The Chronicle of Higher Education* reports that Professor Janet Wright of Dickinson College has only the summer available to do research on wood rats.

Apparently she is concerned that wood rats are disappearing from Pennsylvania and other states for reasons that no one has yet figured out.

When Professor Wright figures it out, there will undoubtedly be an article in some academic journal, which a few people here and there may actually read.

The plight of Professor Wright is only one of a number of personal stories in *The Chronicle of Higher Education* about professors at liberal arts college who are kept so busy teaching during the academic year that the summer is the only time they have available to do their research.

Another whose plight we are presumably supposed to empathize with is a Professor Elmaz Abinader of Mills College who is "writing a three-part performance piece" about the women in her family. It is not clear how a "performance piece" differs from a play or whether this is one of those fine distinctions that keep academic minds occupied.

Professor Michael Womack, a biologist at Macon State College, is out counting mosquitoes for the Federal Emergency

Management Agency. Professor Jane Dirks of Carlow College is doing a study of the ethnic backgrounds of people she encounters while walking her dog. This led to a paper presented at the national meeting of the American Anthropological Association.

Professor Howard Richards of Earlham College says that he is devoting part of his summer vacation to "organizing a whole movement to reconstruct the world."

Reassuring as it is to know that there are things to do to keep academics occupied and off the streets, nevertheless it somehow recalls that old World War II slogan: "Is this trip necessary?"

For the professors themselves, it may be very necessary to keep their resumés from having blank space where there should be publications. Even at liberal arts colleges that emphasize teaching, at least in their brochures, it is increasingly necessary to keep putting things in print, in order to get your contract renewed and, eventually, enter the promised land of tenure.

We of course have no way of knowing how much of Professor Wright's interest in the well-being of Pennsylvania wood rats is due to the pure search for truth and good, any more than we have any way of knowing how much NASA's search for life on other planets is in reality a search for a way to get more money out of the taxpayers on this planet.

At one time, "publish or perish" was the watchword at big research universities but today it is the holy grail from Harvard to Podunk A & M. Criticize the research mania and you will be told that research has produced everything from polio vaccines to the transistor.

A lot of pygmies can hide in the shadows of giants. So the taxpayers are picking up the tab for "research" that serves no other purpose than to fill the library shelves, require more trees to be cut down to produce paper and—not wholly inci-dentally—bring in more money to college and university cof-fers. After all, research grants to support trivialities are just as much hard cash as grants to find a cure for cancer or AIDS.

The costs of these research grants extend far beyond the money directly spent or wasted. In order to free up time for professors to do research, their teaching loads must be re-duced.

When I began teaching in 1962, it was not uncommon in most colleges for a professor to spend 12 hours a week in class and by no means unknown for the average teaching load to be 15 hours. Today, 6 hours a week is the norm in many of those same colleges.

When you cut the average teaching load in half, you are going to need twice as many professors to teach the same number of courses. That means twice as much money for sal-aries, even if the salaries are not going up. But professors' sal-aries have been going up faster than the rate of inflation. That is one of the reasons why tuition has also been going up faster than the rate of inflation.

Research on wood rats and on people you encounter while walking the dog may sound funny—but only if you are not a student, parent or taxpayer who is footing the bill for all this.

LET'S HEAR
IT FOR
UNFAIRNESS!

"Fair" is one of those nice words that make us feel good—no matter how much damage or dangers it leads to. The concept has sunk in so deeply that nothing causes such indignation as the charge that some person, policy or institution has been "unfair."

Yet when I hear educational policies discussed in terms of fairness, my reaction is: Thank God my teachers were unfair to me when I was growing up in Harlem back in the 1940s!

My 7th-grade English teacher, for example, used to require everyone who misspelled a word to write that word 50 times as part of his homework and bring it in the next morning. Misspell three or four words, on top of the rest of your homework, and you had quite an evening ahead of you.

Was this fair? Of course not. Kids on Park Avenue probably heard those words at home far more often than I did. The magazines and books in their homes probably contained many of those words, while my family couldn't afford to subscribe to magazines or buy books.

Fairness was never an option. The only choice was between the temporary unfairness of forcing us to learn things that were a little harder for us to learn and the permanent unfairness of sending us out into the world unprepared and doomed to failure.

Many years later, I happened to run into one of the guys from that school on a street in San Francisco. He was now a psychiatrist and owned a home and property in Napa Valley. If he wanted to live on Park Avenue, I am sure he could afford it now.

As we reminisced about old times and caught up on the things that had happened to us since then, he mentioned that his various secretaries over the years had commented on the fact that he seldom misspelled a word.

"Mine too," I said. "But, if they knew Miss Simon, there would be no mystery as to why we don't misspell words!"

Although I never finished high school and struggled to make ends meet for a few years before going to college, when I took the Scholastic Aptitude Test I scored higher on the verbal portion than the average Harvard student. That was probably why Harvard admitted me. No doubt much of that was due to Miss Simon and other teachers like her who were "unfair" to me.

What if they had been fair to me and my schoolmate? Where would we be today? Maybe in some halfway house—if we were lucky.

Some people say that my philosophy is "tough." But it is life that is tough. My ideas are a piece of cake compared to life.

What about the other kids who went to school in Harlem in the 1940s? Their test scores were very similar to those of white kids in similar neighborhoods, sometimes a shade ahead and sometimes a shade behind, but always in the ballpark—unlike today.

Education is just one of the areas in which the mushy notion of fairness makes those who believe in it feel good about themselves—at the expense of other people's lives.

We are so used to hearing about policemen warning criminals about their right to remain silent that some of the younger generation may not realize that this is something that never existed during three-quarters of the history of the United States.

Back in the 1960s, both the Attorney General of the United States and the Chief Justice of the Supreme Court thought it was unfair that inexperienced and amateurish criminals would make damaging admissions that more savvy crooks and members of crime syndicates would never make. Therefore cops were required to warn everybody, so as to bring the dumbest crook up to the level of the most state-of-the-art mafioso.

There was no thought of the cost of creating this fairness between different categories of criminals. No one asked: How many women are you prepared to see raped, how many neighborhoods terrorized, how many people killed, for the sake of this conception of fairness?

A police chief who tried to caution a conference of judges in 1965 about the consequences of such decisions was literally laughed at—by two Supreme Court justices, among others. How many victims or their widows or orphans would have laughed is another story.

Someone always has to pay the price of fairness, whether in money or in other ways. This straining for an abstract and impossible kind of fairness and justice is one of the most tragic quests of our time.

DOES
IT
ADD UP?

For many years now, American students have been coming in at or near the bottom in international tests of mathematics. Meanwhile, our schools have been entertaining themselves with "new math," "fuzzy math" and everything other than old-fashioned hard-work math that other countries use.

If you want to test your own knowledge of math, here is an example for you. If a school district spends $8,000 per pupil and pays $4,000 for a voucher for each pupil who leaves the public school system, will the total cost of educating all the students go up or down when more students begin using vouchers to transfer out of the public schools?

Take all the time you want. I'll wait. You can even use a pocket calculator if you want to.

If you said that the total cost of educating all the students goes down, then you are a lot smarter than those people who have fallen for the teachers' union argument that vouchers will cost the taxpayers more money. If you went even further and said that the amount of money left to spend on students remaining in the public schools would enable the spending per public school pupil to rise, you are probably in the top one or two percent.

Unfortunately, the dumbing-down of American education has been going on so long that it may now be impossible for many people to see through such flimsy arguments that are made in defense of the status quo in the public schools. These schools' own educational failures in the past may insulate them from the changes they need to make for the future—but which an under-educated public does not realize they need to make.

Seldom, if ever, do students who receive vouchers get more than half of what is spent per pupil in the public schools. Moreover, both voucher schools and charter schools have to provide their own classrooms, while school buildings are provided free to the public school system. So the real disparity in resources is even greater than two-to-one in favor of the public schools.

Despite the deck's being stacked in favor of the public schools, students in voucher schools, charter schools and home schooling almost invariably do at least as well, and usually better, by whatever tests are used.

One of the most hypocritical arguments against vouchers is that the amounts of money given to the students are insufficient to pay for an education in a private school. In reality, tuition at many parochial and other low-budget private schools will in fact be covered by half of what the public schools spend per pupil in many communities. But if those who make this argument are serious, they need only advocate larger amounts of money per voucher. But that is the last thing they will do.

The deck is stacked in favor of the public schools in other ways. Teachers' unions and the public school establishment are already organized for political combat in a way that voucher schools or charter schools cannot be this early in their history. The unions and the public schools are thus able to lobby politicians to impose restrictions and red tape on their rivals.

The education establishment wants the teachers in voucher schools and charter schools to be "certified" as having taken education courses, being unionized and surrounded with all the iron-clad job security that makes it an ordeal to fire even grossly incompetent teachers. Sometimes these restrictions and directives are justified in the name of "fairness," where similar restrictions and directives already apply to the public schools. But this "fairness" argument is completely invalid and misleading.

First, one of the main purposes of voucher schools, charter schools and home schooling is to allow alternative forms of education to escape the bureaucratic rigidities, faddish dogmas and massive red tape that have helped turn too many American public schools into educational disaster areas.

Second, "fairness" is a concept that applies to relations between human beings, not institutions. Institutions are just means to an end. Those institutions that do not serve their purpose—for whatever reason—need to give way to institutions that do.

This does not mean that public schools should be shut down. Rather, they should be forced to compete with alternatives, as other kinds of enterprises have to compete. Whether or not Kodak film is better than Fuji film, both are better than they would be if either had a monopoly.

DIVERSITY
VERSUS
"DIVERSITY"

Sometimes it seems as if "diversity" is going to replace "the" as the most often used word in the English language. Yet the place where this word has become a holy grail—academia— shows less tolerance for genuine diversity of viewpoints than any other American institution.

In a book titled *The College Admissions Mystique*, an admissions office official at Brown University is quoted as setting ideological litmus tests for applicants. An outstanding high school record would not be enough to get admitted, because such records were seen as signs of people who had sold out to traditional ways of thinking—and who envisaged careers in establishment professions. He called such students "Reptilian."

What the admissions official wanted were "with it" kids, socially and politically aware—"bellwethers" who "would have a following later on." In other words, he did not want pillars of society but politically correct pied pipers who could head ideological movements.

In other words, diversity of viewpoints is not welcome. Diversity of physical appearance is the be-all and end-all, but diversity of thought is no more welcome than it has been under the Taliban in Afghanistan.

Such narrowness is not confined to Brown University. Nor

is it confined to admissions offices. Increasingly, ideological litmus tests are applied to the hiring of professors. Candidates for faculty positions report being asked openly ideological questions.

One young scholar who has published very careful and important research that reached politically incorrect conclusions reports being treated with calculated discourtesy and boorishness during job interviews. It was not enough for the cultural commissars to turn him down, they had to try to humiliate him.

This particular scholar has now been hired by a conservative think tank on the east coast. But the real harm that has been done has been done to students who will never learn that there is a factual and reasoned alternative to the one-sided propaganda they will hear in their classrooms.

Incidentally, there is a reason why most of the top-rated think tanks in the world are conservative. When a liberal think tank wants to hire a top scholar in some field, it has to compete with Ivy League universities, Berkeley, Duke, and the like. But conservative think tanks don't have that problem, because the ideological litmus tests in academia bar many conservative scholars from an academic career. Conservative think tanks have little competition when hiring people like the outstanding young man who was dissed at job interviews in places where he was, if anything, over-qualified.

What is remarkable—and appalling—is that so many businessmen keep writing donation checks, some in the millions of dollars, for places where businessmen are demonized by academics who know nothing about business, and where the very possibility that a student applicant might become a businessman is enough reason to blackball him, despite his academic achievements.

Recently, a college student wrote to me that a professor

was shocked to see a book of mine accidentally fall out of his book bag. However, the prof was visibly relieved when the student said that it was just a book that he bought for himself. What this ideological academic had feared was that this book was assigned reading in some course. In other words, four years of steady indoctrination with the left viewpoint might be jeopardized by one little book of essays.

Who knows? It could even lead to diversity.

All this ideological intolerance might seem funny, but it is very serious for those who are true believers on the left and ought to be for those of us who are not. Even if the academic Talibans of the left were correct in all their beliefs about all current issues, it would still be dangerous to leave students unable to weigh and analyze alternatives for themselves, because the issues in the years ahead of them are almost certain to be different. What they were taught will become progressively less relevant and the mental skills that they have not been taught can become a crippling handicap for them—and for our society.

CHOOSING
A
COLLEGE

For many high school seniors and their parents, this is the time of year when colleges let them know if their applications have been accepted. For those who have been chosen, it is now their turn to make their own choices among the colleges that have sent acceptances.

One of the most over-rated factors in these choices are the big names of some colleges and universities. There may be some famous professors at Ivy U., but that doesn't mean much to an undergraduate who is more likely to be taught by graduate students or by temporary "gypsy faculty" who teach introductory courses that the academic stars consider too boring to teach themselves.

For the kind of megabucks tuition that can leave both students and parents in hock for years, this is no bargain. A far better education may be obtained at a good quality college where courses are taught by professors who are competent and available, rather than by the graduate assistants of some research grant baron, to whom undergraduates are a nuisance that he doesn't want to be bothered with.

For minority students, there are further dangers in big-name colleges and universities that want them as warm bodies which visibly demonstrate "diversity" on campus, regardless of whether these students last long enough to graduate.

Despite a recent book by a couple of retired Ivy League university presidents, suggesting that it is imperative that blacks go to elite colleges, whether or not their qualifications match those of the other students there, the cold fact is that it is infinitely better to graduate from Hillsdale College or Birmingham Southern than to flunk out of Berkeley or Columbia. It is also better to get an engineering degree from Cal State at San Luis Obispo than to squeak through some Ivy League school by taking soft courses in subjects that prepare you for nothing but unemployment.

It is a monument to the dedication of many parents that they are willing to take out second mortgages on their homes, in order to pay exorbitant tuition at some prestige institutions. Seldom is it worth it.

Some people point to the fact that students who graduate from big-name colleges earn higher incomes later on. But kids who go horseback riding undoubtedly also go on to earn higher incomes than kids who don't. Does that mean that parents should buy their child a horse, in order to ensure bigger paychecks down the road? Prestige colleges, like horseback riding, are signs of other things that are often the real reason why some people have better chances in life.

Harvard turns out bright students because Harvard takes in bright students—and usually does not ruin them during the four years in between. But that is wholly different from saying that the reason such students do well in later life is because they went to Harvard.

Graduates of Harvey Mudd College go on to receive Ph.D.s a far higher percentage of the time than do the graduates of Harvard. Graduates of Franklin & Marshall College have scored higher on the medical school examination than the graduates of Berkeley.

Parents should also consider the non-academic aspects of

college. Do they really want to send their daughter to a college that has co-ed showers? Many big-name colleges and universities go in for all sorts of dangerous fads like this. Parents can also see their hard-earned tuition money go down the drain when their child is suspended or expelled for a politically incorrect remark.

College guides are often used to help decide where to apply for admissions. There are a couple of guides that should be consulted before deciding where to choose to go after being accepted.

Two guides that tell a lot about the social atmosphere, as well as the curriculum, at colleges across the country are *Choosing the Right College* and the *National Review College Guide*. They are not always in the bookstores and may have to be special ordered. But it is worth the trouble, not simply to avoid wasting money, but also to avoid having a life distorted.

Parents are often regarded as mere obstacles to the student's making his or her own college choices. Not only do some headstrong students feel this way, so do many high school counselors and college admissions office staffers. But it is not their money and not their child—and these know-it-alls are not the ones that will have to pick up the pieces if they steer your child into disaster.

A
PAINFUL
HISTORY

The public in general and parents in particular are shocked from time to time when tests reveal the intellectual incompetence of public school teachers, or when some of the weird fads to which school children have been subjected come to light. But neither the public nor the media seem to see anything beyond the oddities of a particular school or particular teachers.

In reality, there are not only nationwide networks promoting everything from "whole language" to homosexuality in the schools, there is a large body of literature by education gurus—going all the way back to John Dewey in the early 20th century—urging schools away from their traditional role as conveyors of an intellectual heritage toward being "agents of change" in society.

What that means in plain English is that educators should be shaping children to be the kinds of people they want them to be—as distinguished from the kinds of people their parents want them to be. It means that educators should not be so preoccupied with developing intellectual skills and more concerned with inducing in children the kinds of attitudes that would make them receptive to collectivist economic, social and political thinking.

This used to be called progressive education. Its de-emphasis of academics in favor of social engineering, its de-emphasis of teaching in favor of "activities" and "projects," and its de-emphasis of intellectual development in favor of social adjustment and ideological indoctrination are all alive and well today under new names.

An incisive new book titled *Left Behind* by Diane Ravitch, a leading historian of American education, traces the history of the controversies which have raged around educational trends over the past hundred years—"a century of failed school reforms," as Professor Ravitch's subtitle aptly puts it.

These reforms have failed repeatedly because what the public wants—the three R's, for example—conflicts with what the education establishment is determined to do, in its more grandiose vision of its social and political mission. Given this heady feeling about themselves and their role, it is understandable that the education establishment simply dismisses, denigrates and demonizes its critics.

For example, as Professor Ravitch points out, a group of critics who called for rigorous academic standards in the 1930s were likened by John Dewey to religious fundamentalists and were said to be supported by "reactionaries in politics and economics." When the University of Chicago's legendary president, Robert Maynard Hutchins, dared to criticize progressive education, the head of Columbia Teachers College said: "Dr. Hutchins stands near to Hitler." This is the level at which too many educators continue to answer critics today.

American leaders of the progressive education movement, including its supreme guru John Dewey, went to the Soviet Union in the 1920s, when their theories were being put into practice on a mass scale there. They came back gushing with praise for Soviet education, as well as other aspects of Soviet society.

It was only after progressive education failed to turn out

competently educated people that Stalin purged its advocates—and Dewey and others then began to develop some belated skepticism about the Soviet Union in general.

This whole story was played out once again, decades later, in China under Mao during the "cultural revolution." Here again, these romantic theories led to gross incompetence and China was forced to return to practices that were not so romantic, but which produced results.

Ignorant of history, undaunted by facts, and undeterred by logic, American educators have subjected generations of American children to the same practices, with the same dismal results. Our children now regularly come in at or near the bottom in international tests, especially in no-nonsense subjects like math.

In a sense, this is not failure, but success at a different agenda. It took progressive education generations to achieve complete hegemony in our schools and teachers' colleges. Diane Ravitch's *Left Behind* traces how it happened and the assumptions and goals behind it. After you read this book, the strange things that go on in our schools today may not seem inexplicable any more.

What this book demonstrates is that the decline of American education was no accident, but the by-product of a mindset and an agenda with a long pedigree.

"FORCED
TO
VOLUNTEER"

The term "liberal" originally referred politically to those who wanted to liberate people—mainly from the oppressive power of government. That is what it still means in various European countries or in Australia and New Zealand. It is the American meaning that is unusual: People who want to increase the power of government, in order to accomplish various social goals.

Typical of what liberalism has come to mean in the United States today is a proposal by California Governor Gray Davis that the state's colleges and universities make "community service" a graduation requirement. His plan immediately won the unconditional support of the state's largest newspaper, the liberal *Los Angeles Times*. There was no sense of irony in its editorial claiming beneficial effects for "students who are forced to volunteer."

Forced to volunteer. That is the Orwellian notion to which contemporary liberalism has sunk.

"What could be wrong," the *L.A. Times* asks, "with teaching students, as the governor puts it, that 'a service ethic . . . [has] lasting value in California?'" A community service requirement "could reap a valuable return in a new generation of civically minded citizens."

Here we get to the heart of the so-called community service idea. Its central purpose is to create a certain set of attitudes in the students. It is compulsory submission to state-sponsored propaganda for the liberals' vision of the world. That is what students must be "forced to volunteer" for.

What is wrong with the idea of a free people, using their own time as they see fit, for those things that matter most to them, instead of being pawns in a propaganda program more in keeping with what happens in totalitarian societies? What is wrong with each individual defining for himself or herself what being civic minded means, instead of having the government define it and impose it?

In a country where more than 90 million people already volunteer for civic projects of their own choosing, why must students be drafted to become "volunteers" for environmentalism or other causes dear to the heart of the *Los Angeles Times* or Governor Davis? The casual arrogance of those who define for other people what is a "community service" is breathtaking.

Environmentalism can—and does—reach extremes where it is a disservice to the community. Programs which subsidize the homeless lifestyle can turn able-bodied men into idle nuisances on streets across America. We need not try to force liberals to believe this. But they have no right to use the educational system to force young people to submit to propaganda for their version.

The totalitarian mind-set behind the liberal vision shows through in innumerable ways. There are no institutions in America where free speech is more severely restricted than in our politically correct colleges and universities, dominated by liberals.

Students who openly disagree with the left-wing vision that they are being taught in class can find themselves facing lower grades and insults from the professor in front of their classmates and friends. Offend the hyper-sensitivities of any of the sacred cow groups on campus—even inadvertently—and stronger punishments, ranging up to suspension or expulsion, can follow.

On the other hand, if minorities, homosexuals or radical feminists want to shout down speakers they don't like or engage in vandalism or other mob actions to promote their agendas, that's OK.

Campus ideological conformity extends to faculty hiring and even the inviting of outside speakers to give talks on campus. There are scholars of international distinction who would never be offered a faculty appointment in most Ivy League colleges and universities today because they do not march in step ideologically. You can find a four-leaf clover faster than you can find a Republican in most sociology departments or English departments.

If the liberals are teaching any civics lesson with all this, it is that power is what matters—including the power to force people to keep their thoughts to themselves, if those thoughts do not conform to the liberal vision.

Community "volunteer" work is only the latest in a series of uses of schools and colleges to propagandize political correctness, instead of teaching individuals to think for themselves. If liberals do not understand that this is the antithesis of liberation, that makes it all the more urgent for the rest of us to recognize that fact and that danger.

DRUGGING
CHILDREN

The motto used to be: "Boys will be boys." Today, the motto seems to be: "Boys will be medicated."

Of nearly 20 million prescriptions written last year for drugs to treat "attention deficit hyperactivity disorder," most were for children and most of those children were boys. This is part of a growing tendency to treat boyhood as a pathological condition that requires a new three R's—repression, reeducation and Ritalin.

Some schools have gone to such extremes as banning recess, since boys tend to be boisterous at recess. Competitive sports are likewise banned or made non-competitive, sometimes by banning winning and losing. An aptly titled book, *The War Against Boys* by Christina Hoff Sommers, catalogs the amazing array of things that schools do to keep boys from being boys.

Some of this is being pushed by propaganda from radical feminists who want boys to be like girls. Their dogmas declare that the behavior usually seen in boys is a result of society's indoctrinating them with a male role stereotype. The answer? "We need to raise boys like we raise girls," according to Gloria Steinem. Gloria Allred is more specific, "we need to socialize boys at an earlier age, perhaps to be playing with dolls." Some schools have followed such advice, even to the point of encouraging boys to wear dresses.

Despite the radical feminist dogma that sex differences are created by society, and that maleness in particular needs to be changed by society, a growing body of scientific evidence shows that boys and girls differ from day one, beginning in the womb, before society has had anything to do with them. The radical feminist response to such evidence? They say such research should be banned! Even without such bans, their mindless dogmas prevail over scientific evidence and pervade the education establishment.

Meanwhile, there are drug companies making well over a hundred million dollars a year each by selling drugs for "attention deficit hyperactivity disorder." Knowing a good thing, they are now not only advertising these drugs to doctors and school officials, but are also trying to gain more widespread acceptance from parents by running ads aimed at mothers through such outlets as the *Ladies' Home Journal* and 30-second TV commercials.

Yet how does "attention deficit hyperactivity disorder" differ from just being bored and restless with the mindless stuff being served up in school? The question is not simply how does it differ in principle, when diagnosed by high-level specialists, but how does it differ in practice when the term is applied by lower-level people in the local schools?

A large body of research shows that high-IQ students are often bored and alienated from school. These include Einstein and India's self-taught mathematical genius Ramanujan. Fortunately, there was no Ritalin around when they were children, to drug them into passivity—and perhaps into mediocrity.

No doubt life is easier for teachers when everyone sits around quietly, not making any waves. But schools do not exist to make teaching easy. Moreover, some of the brightest youngsters have some of the strongest reactions to what they see and hear.

According to a study of gifted children by Professor Ellen Winner of Boston College: "These children have been reported to show unusually intense reactions to noise, pain, and frustration." Biographies of some famous people show the same pattern.

Einstein, for example, had tantrums until he was seven years old. In one outburst, he threw a stool at his tutor, who fled and was never seen again. According to a biography of the great pianist Arthur Rubinstein, he became fixated on his family's piano as a toddler and, whenever he was asked to leave the room where it was kept, he screamed and wept. When his father bought him a violin to play, he reacted by smashing it.

Too many parents have gone along when schools have wanted their children drugged. When some parents have objected, they have been threatened with charges of child neglect for not letting drugs be used to control their youngster's behavior.

Belatedly, in response to many revelations of the widespread use of Ritalin and other drugs in schools, some states have begun to pass laws restricting what school personnel and social workers can push parents to do. A new law in Connecticut will limit such medical advice to doctors. It's about time. That common sense restriction should be nationwide. Schools have too many busybodies posing as "experts."

GOODBYE TO SARA AND BENJAMIN?

Recently a couple of dear friends visited us, bringing with them their six-year-old twins, Sara and Benjamin. These are some of the loveliest children you could meet—not just in appearance, but in their behavior. They are the kinds of kids you can see in Norman Rockwell paintings, but less and less in the real world.

Now Sara and Benjamin are going off to public school and it is painful to imagine what they might be like a year from now. Most people are unaware how much time and effort the public schools—and some private schools—are putting into undermining the values and understanding that children were taught by their parents and re-orienting them toward the avant-garde vision of the world that is fashionable in the educational establishment.

Today's educators believe it is their job to introduce children like Sara and Benjamin to sex when and in whatever manner they see fit, regardless of what the children's parents might think. Raw movies of both heterosexuals and homosexuals in action are shown in elementary schools.

Weaning children away from their parents' influence in general is a high priority in many schools. Children sit in what is called a "magic circle" and talk about all sorts of personal things, with the rule being that they are not to repeat any of these things to anyone outside this magic circle. Sometimes they are explicitly told not to repeat what is said to their parents.

Some handbooks for teachers warn against letting parents know the specifics of what is being done and provide strategies for side-stepping parental questions and concerns. Glowing generalities and high-sounding names like "gifted and talented" programs conceal what are nothing more than brainwashing operations to convert the children from their parents' values to the values preferred by educational gurus.

Right and wrong are among the earliest targets of these programs. "There is no 'right' way or 'right' age to have life experiences," one widely used textbook says. Another textbook tells children that they may listen to their parents "if you are interested in their ideas." But, if there is a difference of opinion, parent and child alike should see the other's point of view "as different, not wrong."

Sara and Benjamin are only six years old and are going into the first grade. Will any of this apply to them? Yes. There is a textbook designed for children ranging from pre-school to the third grade, which tells children about their rights and about asserting those rights to parents. Whenever "things happen you don't like," you have "the right to be angry without being afraid of being punished" it says.

In other words, don't take any guff off mommy and daddy. Who are they? As another textbook says, parents are just "ordinary people with faults and weaknesses and insecurities and problems just like everyone else." In many of the textbooks, movies and other material used in schools, parents are depicted as old-fashioned people who are out of touch and full of hang-ups.

What these smug underminers of parents fail to understand is that the relationship of a child to his or her parents is the most extraordinary relationship anyone is likely to have with another human being. No one else is likely to sacrifice so much for another person's wellbeing. If the avant-garde ideas taught to children in schools blow up in their faces, it is the parents who will be left to pick up the pieces, not the glib gurus.

Most of the classroom teachers who carry out such educational fashions and fetishes have no idea where they originated or what their underlying purpose is. In reality, many of the techniques and strategies used to break down the child's values, personality and modesty are straight out of totalitarian brainwashing practices from the days of Stalin and Mao.

That is the origin, for example, of the personal journals that children are required to keep in schools all across the United States. These journals are not educational. Gross mistakes in spelling, grammar and usage are ignored, not corrected. These journals are gateways to the psyche and the first step in manipulating little minds.

As our friends departed and went off to enroll their children in the public schools, I could not help wondering if I had seen Sara and Benjamin for the last time. Would they still be the same sweet children after they have been used as guinea pigs by those who claim to be trying to educate them?

SUCCESS
CONCEALING
FAILURE

Among the many clever and misleading defenses of our failing educational system is the assertion that our universities are among the highest rated in the world and Americans consistently win a disproportionate number of Nobel Prizes. Both these claims are accurate—and irrelevant.

While Americans won the lion's share of Nobel Prizes in 1999, not one of these winners was actually born in the United States. If people born and raised elsewhere choose to come here and use their talents, fine. But do not claim their achievements as some vindication of the American educational system.

On the contrary, the painful question must be faced: Why were a quarter of a billion native-born Americans unable to win a single Nobel Prize in 1999, when a relative handful of naturalized Americans won so many? This is not a vindication but an indictment of our educational system.

The top-rated American universities owe much to the generosity of American donors and the largess of the American government, which enable them to attract top scholars from around the world. It is research, rather than teaching, which determines world rankings, and our well-financed Ph.D.-granting universities are unquestionably among the best at research.

However, when you look at who gets degrees in what, again the picture is very disturbing as regards the track record of the schools and colleges that prepare students to enter these top-rated institutions.

Less than half the Ph.D.s in engineering and mathematics awarded by American universities are received by Americans. Even more revealing, there is a systematic relationship between the difficulty of the subject and the percentage of American doctorates which go to Americans.

In a mushy and undemanding field like education, more than four out of five of the doctorates go to Americans. It is when you start getting into the physical sciences that the proportion drops to barely half and when you get into engineering and math that Americans become a minority among American university Ph.D.s.

Foreign graduate students predominate so heavily in difficult subjects that a common complaint across the country is that undergraduate math courses are being taught by people whose English is hard to understand, quite aside from the difficulty of learning the subject itself.

Yes, our top universities are the cream of the crop. They are so good that people educated in American schools and colleges cannot hold their own with foreign students who go there.

The period during which American public schools have had declining test scores has coincided with the period during which Americans were increasingly displaced by foreigners in the graduate programs of our top universities.

In every field surveyed by the Council of Graduate Schools, the proportion of graduate degrees in the United States going to Americans has declined over a period of two decades, with the worst declines being in the more demanding subjects.

A closer look at those Americans who do still hold their own in difficult fields is also revealing. Nearly 22 percent of all Ph.D.s in engineering received by Americans are received by Asian Americans. Here is the group that is most out of step with the prevailing easy-going education, with its emphasis on "self-esteem" and other mushy fads. Again, this is not a vindication but an indictment of what is being done in our public schools.

Ironically, people who go ballistic when minorities are "under-represented," relative to their percentage of the population, whether among college degree recipients or in various professions, remain strangely silent when the whole American population is under-represented among those receiving post-graduate degrees in science, math and engineering in their own country.

Such under-representation might be understandable if the United States were some Third World country just entering the world of modern science and technology. It is staggering in a country whose people led the world in such things in the recent past. Clearly something has gone very wrong in our educational system.

Our current world leadership in science and technology, like our leadership in Nobel Prizes, owes much to people who never went through the dumbed-down education in American schools and colleges. Many come from countries which spend far less per pupil than we do but get far better results for their money.

THE
OLD
NEIGHBORHOOD

Recently I got together with a guy who grew up in my old neighborhood in Harlem, around 145th St. and St. Nicholas Avenue. As we talked about the old days, the world that we discussed seemed like something from another planet, compared to today.

There have been many good changes but, on net balance, it is doubtful whether kids growing up in our old neighborhood today have as much chance of rising out of poverty as we did.

That is not because poverty is worse today. It is not. My friend remembers times when his father would see that the children were fed but would go to bed without eating dinner himself. There were other times when his father would walk to work in downtown Manhattan—several miles away—rather than spend the nickel it took to ride the subway in those days.

Things were not quite that grim for me, but my family was by no means middle class. None of the adults had gotten as far as the seventh grade. Down South, before we moved to New York, most of the places where we lived did not come with frills like electricity or hot running water.

Some people have said that my rising from such a background was unique. But it was not. Many people from that same neighborhood went on to have professional careers and I am by no means either the best known or the most financially successful of them.

Harry Belafonte came out of the same building where my old school-mate lived. One of the guys from the neighborhood was listed in one of the business magazines as having a net worth of more than $200 million today.

If anyone had told me then that one of the guys on our block was going to grow up to be a multi-millionaire, I would have wondered what he was drinking.

Not everybody made it. One of my old buddies was found shot dead some years ago, in what looked like a drug deal gone bad. But many people from that neighborhood went on to become doctors, lawyers, and academics—at least one of whom became a dean and another a college president.

My old school-mate retired as a psychiatrist and was living overseas, with servants, until recently deciding to return home. But home now is not Harlem. He lives out in the California wine country.

Why are the kids in that neighborhood today not as likely to have such careers—especially after all the civil rights "victories" and all the billions of dollars worth of programs to get people out of poverty?

What government programs gave was transient and superficial. What they destroyed was more fundamental.

My old school-mate recalls a teacher seeing him eating his brown bag lunch in our school lunchroom. A forerunner of a later generation of busybodies, she rushed him over to the line where people were buying their lunches and gave some sign to the cashier so that he would not have to pay.

Bewildered at the swift chain of events, he sat down to eat and then realized what had happened. He had been given charity! He gagged on the food and then went to the toilet to spit it out. He went hungry that day because his brown bag lunch had been thrown out. He had his pride—and that pride would do more for him in the long run than any lunches.

His father also had his pride. He tore to shreds a question-naire that the school had sent home to find out about their students' living conditions. Today, even middle-class parents with Ph.D.s tamely go along with this kind of meddling. Moreover, people like his father have been made superfluous by the welfare state—and made to look like chumps if they pass it up.

What the school we went to gave us was more precious than gold. It was an education. That was what schools did in those days.

We didn't get mystical talk about the rain forests and no-body gave us condoms or chirped about "diversity." And no-body would tolerate our speaking anything in school but the king's English.

After finishing junior high school, my friend was able to pass the test to get into the Bronx High School of Science, where the average IQ was 135, and yours truly passed the same test to get into Stuyvesant High School, another selective pub-lic school that today's community "leaders" denounce as "elit-ist."

The rest is history. But it is a history that today's young blacks are unlikely to hear—and are less likely to repeat.

WASTING
MINDS

Menlo-Atherton High School in an affluent California community is considered to be very good academically, at least by current standards, in an era of dumbed-down education. Yet its problems are all too typical of what is wrong with American education today.

A gushing account of the free breakfast program and other giveaways to lower-income students who attend this high school recently appeared in the *San Francisco Chronicle*, while the *Wall Street Journal* presented a sympathetic account of the school's attempt to teach science to students of very disparate abilities in the same classroom.

Even more revealing, the villains in this story—as seen by both the educators and by the reporter for the *Wall Street Journal*—are those parents who want their children to get the best education they can, instead of being used as guinea pigs for social and educational experiments.

Creating a science class that included students of very different levels of ability and motivation was one of these experiments. These disparities were especially great in this particular school, since its students come from both highly-educated, high-income families in Silicon Valley and low-income Hispanic and other minority families from the wrong side of the local freeway. Moreover, they were fed into the high school from their respective neighborhood schools with very different standards.

The science class turned out to be a disaster. While the principal admired the good intentions behind it, he also admitted "it was almost impossible to pull off in real life. The disparity was too great." Yet the science teacher blamed the ending of this experiment on affluent parents who "really didn't give it a chance" and the principal spoke of the "heat" he got from such parents, who "thought their kids were being held back by the other kids, that their children's chances for MIT or Stanford were being hampered."

This was seen as a public relations problem, rather than as a perfectly legitimate complaint from parents who took their responsibilities for their children's education seriously—more seriously than the "educators" who tried to be social workers or world savers.

In a school where 40 percent of the children are Hispanic and 38 percent are white, sharp income and cultural divisions translate into racial or ethnic divisions plainly visible to the naked eye. This also arouses the ideological juices and emotional expressions of resentment, both inside and outside the school.

Stanford University's school of education is reluctant to send its graduates to teach at Menlo-Atherton High School because the latter doesn't make enough effort to overcome "inequalities" and uses politically incorrect "tracking" by ability "to keep affluent kids protected from the other kids."

In other words, a school that takes in fifteen-year-olds from radically different backgrounds is supposed to come up with some miracle that can make them all equal in ability, despite fifteen years of prior inequality in education and upbringing. Somehow, there are always magic solutions out there, just waiting to be found, like eggs at an Easter egg hunt.

Make-believe equality at the high school level fools nobody, least of all the kids. White kids at Menlo-Atherton refer to the non-honors courses as "ghetto courses," while a black kid who enrolled in honors courses had his friends demand to know why he was taking "that white-boy course."

If you are serious about education, then you need to start a lot earlier than fifteen years old to give each child a decent shot at life in the real world, as distinguished from make-believe equality while in school. Ability grouping or "tracking"—so hated by the ideological egalitarians—is one of the best ways of doing that.

If you were a black kid in a Harlem school back in the 1940s, and you had both the desire and the ability to get a first-rate education, it was there for you in the top-ability class. The kids who were not interested in education, or who preferred to spend their time fighting or clowning around, were in other classes and did not hold back the ones who were ready to learn.

Our egalitarian dogmas prevent that today, destroying low-income and minority youngsters' opportunities for real equality. A mind is indeed a terrible thing to waste, especially when it is the only avenue to a better life.

THE
"NON-PROFIT"
HALO

You may never have heard of the University of Phoenix, but it has more students than Harvard, Yale and Notre Dame—combined.

There is a reason you probably have not heard of the University of Phoenix. It represents a new development in higher education and one that the establishment does not welcome.

The vast majority of colleges and universities are non-profit organizations, but the University of Phoenix is not. To some people, non-profit organizations have a sort of halo around them. It is another example of the power of mere words that the fact that one organization's income is called "profit" and another's income is not makes such a huge difference to so many people, including the government, which treats non-profit organizations differently.

Officials of non-profit organizations are not volunteers donating their time. The average university president has a six-figure salary and many also get free use of a big, expensive house. There are three university presidents whose annual salaries and benefits exceed half a million dollars a year each. In addition, it is not uncommon for top professors in medical schools to earn even more than their university presidents, while college athletic coaches often have the highest incomes of all.

Nevertheless, it is considered shocking in genteel academia that the University of Phoenix is legally set up as an organization that is out to make a buck, even though most of us get our food, our shelter and our medical care from such organizations. Indeed, those of us who were not born rich and who don't want to live on welfare are out there every working day trying to make a buck.

Ironically, the real reason for the opposition to the University of Phoenix is precisely because it would threaten the money coming in to conventional, non-profit colleges and universities. As a new institution, Phoenix does not have to do all the costly things that conventional academic institutions have been doing for many generations, so it can charge lower tuition.

For example, it does not have the expenses of a huge campus, a football stadium and dormitories. Its students are largely adults scattered all around the country, who communicate with the university on the Internet. The University of Phoenix also does not have to have the huge and costly libraries that most universities have because it provides electronic access to more than 3,000 journals, while the need for books is not nearly as great, because this university specializes primarily in business courses, and so does not need to cover everything from astronomy to zoology.

What an economist might call greater efficiency is depicted by conventional colleges and universities as "unfair competition." Unfortunately, the various licensing and accrediting agencies have requirements which reflect the situation of liberal arts colleges and universities catering to a younger clientele, studying a wider variety of subjects.

Worse yet, political pressures from the existing educational establishment add to the hurdles facing any fundamentally new academic institutions that do not take on the costly ways of operating that the old ones use, including tenure for professors and adolescent activities and lifestyles for the students.

I have no idea what the quality of education is at the University of Phoenix—and it is none of my business. It is the business of the university's 53,000 students and whatever new students it may get wherever it is allowed to compete with conventional non-profit colleges and universities. It is the business of employers who are thinking of hiring University of Phoenix graduates and it is the business of postgraduate institutions who need to judge their qualifications for admissions.

Much of the enormous costliness and irresponsible self-indulgence of the academic world comes from the fact that it has neither accountability nor competition. It has little or no incentive to do things efficiently and every incentive to appease every campus constituency by giving them their own turf, at the expense of the taxpayers, donors and tuition-paying parents.

Accountability is so remote in academia that conventional colleges and universities need all the competition they can get. The academic establishment's fear and resentment of the University of Phoenix is a sign of how much some real competition is needed. But such competition may be stifled by arcane laws that serve to protect the academic dinosaurs.

DO
FACTS
MATTER?

Recently a young black man sent a thoughtful e-mail to me. Among his kind comments was an expression of sympathy for the racism that he thought blacks of my generation must have experienced in going through college.

In reality, it is his generation of blacks who have encountered more racial hostility on campus than mine. But his was an understandable mistake, given how little attention is paid to accuracy in history and how often history is used as just a propaganda tool in current controversies.

My college and early postgraduate education took place during the 1950s—that decade before the political left brought its light into the supposed darkness of the world. During the decade of the 1950s I attended four academic institutions—a year and a half at a black institution, Howard University, three years at Harvard, where I graduated, nine months at Columbia, where I received a master's degree, and a summer at New York University.

I cannot recall a single racist word or deed at any of these institutions. The closest thing to a racist remark was made about a student from England who was referred to as "nasty, British and short." It was I who made that remark.

My first encounter with racism on campus came toward the end of my four years of teaching at Cornell in the 1960s—

and it erupted after black students were admitted under lower standards than white students and were permitted to engage in disruptions that would have gotten anyone else suspended or expelled. I was not the target of any of these racist incidents, which were directed against black students. I received a standing ovation in the last class I taught at Cornell.

One of the black students at Cornell moved in with my wife and me for a while, because she was afraid of both the black militants and those whites who were increasingly bitter about both the trouble that the militants were causing and the way the administration was catering to them. This backlash was not peculiar to Cornell, but developed on many campuses and became so widely known over the years that it acquired a name—"the new racism."

In the late 1980s, for example, a dean at Middlebury College reported that—for the first time in her 19 years at that institution—she was getting requests from white students not to be housed with black room mates. People who had taught at Berkeley for similar periods of time likewise reported that they were seeing racist graffiti and hate mail for the first time. More than two-thirds of graduating seniors at Stanford said that racial tensions had increased during their years on campus.

All this is the direct opposite of what you might be led to believe by the politically correct history or theory of race in America. The endlessly repeated mantra of "diversity" implies that such things as group quotas and group identity programs improve race relations. Quotas are often thought to be necessary, in order to create a "critical mass" of black students on campus, so that they can feel sufficiently comfortable socially to do their best academic work.

That there are various opinions on such things is not surprising. What ought to be surprising—indeed, shocking—is that these social dogmas have been repeated for decades, with no serious effort to test whether or not they are true.

When elite liberal institutions like Stanford, Berkeley and the Ivy League colleges have been scenes of racial apartheid and racial tensions on campus, have more conservative institutions that have resisted quotas and preferences been better or worse in these respects? My impression has been that they have been better. But the real problem is that we must rely on impressions because all the vast research money and time that have gone into racial issues have still not even addressed this key question that goes to the heart of the dogmas pervading academia today.

Over a period of more than three decades, during the first half of the 20th century, 34 black students from Dunbar High School in Washington were admitted to Amherst College. Of these, about three-fourths graduated and more than one-fourth of these graduates were Phi Beta Kappa. But there were never more than a handful of black students at Amherst during that era—nothing like a "critical mass."

Is this evidence conclusive? No. But it is evidence—and the political left avoids evidence like the plague.

DO FACTS
MATTER?
PART II

The history of the education of blacks in America has become politicized to the point where it is barely recognizable as history, rather than as an arsenal of horror stories to be used in the political wars of today. Many of these horror stories are true, even if increasingly dated, but there is an almost complete disregard of other important aspects of the history of black education that are also true.

Yes, Governor Wallace stood in front of the entrance to a building on the campus of the University of Alabama, in order to try to prevent black students from being enrolled. Yes, white mobs jeered and attacked the first black college students to enroll in previously segregated Southern colleges and universities. Worse, such mobs tried to impede the enrolment of black youngsters in public schools in various Northern cities, as well as in the South.

But the real story is that all these efforts failed. And they failed because the American government, with the support of the American people, would not stand for letting them succeed. More important, these episodes were just episodes in a much larger epic.

During the era of slavery, it was illegal to teach slaves to read and write, throughout the Western Hemisphere. In parts of the antebellum South, it was also illegal for free blacks to be educated and there was no provision for them to be educated in much of the North. Yet the census of 1850 showed that more than half of the 500,000 free blacks were able to read and write.

How did that happen? It happened because they set up their own schools, even in places where such schools were illegal and had to operate underground. What an insult to their memory when blacks in ghetto schools today who want to get an education are accused by their peers of "acting white"! Black people risked jail to set up schools for their children before the Civil War.

One of the most inspiring and heroic episodes in the history of black education in America came after the Civil War, when numerous white school teachers from the North went South to teach the children of the freed slaves, often under the auspices of religious organizations—and in defiance of ostracism by Southern whites. Voluntary and privately financed efforts to educate blacks were so widespread that it was 1916 before there were as many blacks in public high schools as in private high schools.

Blacks themselves went to extraordinary lengths to create an educated class. The building of Tuskeegee Institute, literally with the students' own hands, is a story seldom told, because it was done under the leadership of Booker T. Washington, who is not politically correct today. He is excoriated by those who have never bothered to study the facts about the man or his times.

As far back as 1899, the one black academic high school in Washington scored higher on standardized tests than two of the three white high schools in the nation's capital. In the decades that followed, its graduates went on to college at a higher rate than that of white Americans. From this school came the first black federal judge, the first black general to lead men in combat, the first black Cabinet member, the first black elected to the Senate and many other firsts. All this from one school.

Yet this story too is seldom mentioned today, because it too was done in ways that are not considered politically correct. Far from looking inward at the ghetto or being Afro-centric or teaching—or even tolerating—"black English," it opened the students' minds to a wider world of culture, including requiring the learning of Latin and the study of the classics.

Facts about other successful black schools, past and present, get very little attention from the intelligentsia because the stories of these schools would not forward the agendas of the left. In short, history is treated as just the continuation of politics by other means.

But for anyone who is serious about wanting to see black youngsters get a better education, the story of what works and what doesn't work is more important than what is fashionable and not fashionable in the education establishment, or what is or is not considered politically correct among the intelligentsia, politicians, the education establishment or the media.

The real question is: How many people are serious about improving the education of black youngsters, as distinguished from advancing the many other agendas that stand in the way of that improvement?

PART V
LEGAL
ISSUES

PROPERTY
RITES

With police on hand to try to maintain order, the Loudon County (Virginia) board of supervisors recently imposed severe restrictions on the building of homes, despite angry protesters. The board's plan allows only one house to be built for every 10 acres in some places and for every 20 or 50 acres in other places.

Opponents of these restrictions accused the supervisors of violating their property rights. One of their signs read: "Thou shalt not steal."

Property rights are one of the most misunderstood things in law and one of the most disregarded things in politics. The vast amount of land that the Loudon County supervisors are micro-managing does not belong to them or to Loudon County. It belongs to its respective individual owners.

According to the Constitution of the United States, the government cannot take private property without compensation. However, judges have been letting governments get away with doing just that for about half a century now. So long as the title to the property remains in the hands of its owners, the courts let local, state and federal governments do pretty much what they please, even if that destroys much of the value of the property.

From an economic point of view, there is no real difference

between confiscating half of someone's property and reducing its value by half. When county officials drastically restrict the uses to which land can be put, that land becomes less valuable on the market. A farmer cannot sell his land to someone who wants to build an apartment complex if the county regulations make it illegal to build an apartment complex.

When the use of land is restricted to ways that only the wealthy can afford, that eliminates a major part of the demand for that land—and a major part of its value. Land use laws are just one way that governments can confiscate much of the value of private property without having to compensate the owner. Where there are stringent rent control laws, as in New York City, the cost of the services that a landlord is required to provide can exceed the rents he is allowed to collect, so that an apartment building can end up with a zero value—or even a negative value.

That is why thousands of buildings in New York have been simply abandoned by their owners and ended up boarded up. The entire value of the building has been destroyed by government, without compensation.

One of the reasons property rights do not get all the protection that the Constitution prescribes is that they are seen as special benefits to the affluent, which must give way to the general welfare. The old leftist phrase "property rights versus human rights" summarizes this mindset.

This ignores the value of property rights to the society as a whole, including people who own no property. Most Americans do not own agricultural land, but they get an abundance of food at affordable prices because farmers own both land and its produce as their private property, and therefore have incentives to produce far more efficiently than in countries where the land is owned by the government. The Soviet Union was a classic example of the latter, with hungry people despite an abundance of fertile land, inefficiently used under government control.

Loudon County illustrates another danger in political confiscation of private property. It is precisely the wealthy and the affluent who gain by restricting other people's property rights. Although the average rich person—by definition—has more money than other people, the non-rich often have far more wealth in the aggregate, simply because they are more numerous.

In a free market with undiluted property rights, the non-rich would out-bid the rich for much land and use that land in ways that suit the circumstances of ordinary people. For example, grand estates would be broken up into smaller plots for more modest homes or used for building apartment complexes. That is what the affluent and the wealthy strive to prevent by government-imposed restrictions on land use. Such restrictions also increase the value of the existing estates of the rich.

California pioneered in such restrictions, years ago, which is why California real estate prices and apartment rents are out of sight. But Loudon County is one of many other places that are now catching up, using the same legalistic techniques and the same political rhetoric about the environment, preventing "sprawl," and other pieties that beguile the gullible.

LOVE
THOSE
KILLERS!

Most of us were horrified to learn that Andrea Yates had killed five of her own children by drowning them—one at a time—in a bathtub. But that may be because we are not among the morally anointed. Big time celebrities like Rosie O'Donnell and Today Show hostess Katie Couric apparently see things differently.

"I felt such overwhelming empathy for her of what it must have been like for her to do that," said Rosie O'Donnell. "When you've been on the edge you can understand what it's like to go over."

Katie Couric on the Today Show seemed likewise to think the big issue was Mrs. Yates' psyche. She said: "Mrs. Yates, after you drowned your five children, how did that make you feel?"

The Today Show put on the screen information showing where to send donations to the legal defense fund for Andrea Yates. In Houston, the local chapter of the National Organization for Women formed something called "The Andrea Yates Support Coalition" and is planning to raise money for her defense.

This has apparently become a so-called woman's issue because the claim is being made that Mrs. Yates suffered from postpartum depression and that either that or the drugs she had to take caused her to kill her children. But of course the reason we hold trials is to find out which claims by either side can stand up in court.

The judge has slapped a gag order on the attorneys in this case, in order to prevent pre-trial publicity from biasing the jury. But, in reality, that just means that the public will hear only Andrea Yates' side of the story before the trial. We will of course never hear the children's side of the story.

Unfortunately, the vogue of leaping to the defense of killers is not limited to women or even to the United States. Just this summer, two teenage boys who had sadistically murdered a two-year old toddler in Britain when they were ten years old were released from prison—and given new identities, so that they would not suffer any bad consequences from members of the public who were not as much in tune with current non-judgmental fashions.

What other people might suffer from these young killers in the course of another half century or more of their lives did not seem to raise nearly as much concern. Shrinks said that they were no danger to others—which is what shrinks said about some of the American teenagers who later killed their schoolmates in shooting sprees.

At a cost of about $2 million to the British taxpayers, the young British killers and their families have been set up in three-bedroom homes. They have even been given spending money, with which one of the parents has bought a car.

Even before being released from "imprisonment"—in facilities without bars but with TV and other amenities, including karate lessons and spending money for Christmas—the young killers were allowed out on supervised furlough to see sports events and even visit shopping malls. It was at a shopping mall that they had lured the little toddler away and then tortured him to death.

The foreman of the jury that convicted them recalls seeing

the terrible pictures of the little toddler's body and then catching the eye of one of the young killers—who smirked in the courtroom. However, the politically correct line in Britain, as in the United States, is that expressed by a "penal reform" advocate, who said: "If children do something wrong, they should be dealt with through the care system and not the criminal justice system."

Meanwhile, the liberal media in England has vilified the mother of the murdered child, who has protested these boys' early release and the posh life provided for them and their families. The media "compared her unfavourably with more forgiving mothers," according to *The Guardian* newspaper. Apparently all mothers should be non-judgmental about their babies' sadistic young killers.

Back in the 1960s, it was considered eccentric, at least, when Norman Mailer took up the cause of a convicted murderer and managed to get him released from behind bars. It was no doubt considered somewhat more than eccentric by a man that the ex-con killed after being released. But today, what was once considered eccentric is par for the course in certain elite circles.

Outcries of outrage from the public only confirm the anointed in their own smug sense of being special—nobler and wiser than the common herd. What a price to pay so that some people can feel more non-judgmental than thou or simply affirm within their own little coterie that they are one of Us instead of one of Them.

MICROSOFT
AND ANTI-TRUST
"LAW"

The biggest question about anti-trust law is whether there really is any such thing. There are anti-trust theories and anti-trust rhetoric, as well as judicial pronouncements on anti-trust. But there is very little that could be called law in the full sense of rules known in advance and applied consistently.

Federal judge Thomas Penfield Jackson's recent ruling in the anti-trust case against Microsoft is a classic example of lawless "law." Just what specific law did Microsoft violate and how did they violate it?

While Judge Jackson's long pronouncement opens with a brief reference to sections 1 and 2 of the Sherman anti-trust act, this is little more than a passing formality. What follows is a lengthy exposition of theoretical conclusions about the economic meaning of Microsoft's actions. Is Microsoft supposed to have violated a theory or to have violated a law? What was it that they should have known in advance not to do?

Courts have declared laws against vagrancy to be void because of their vagueness, which gives the individual no clear understanding of just what they are supposed to do or not do. But vagrancy laws are a model of clarity compared to Sections 1 and 2 of the Sherman Act, which forbid conspiracies "in restraint of trade" or any "attempt to monopolize."

Just what does that mean? It means whatever Judge Thomas Penfield Jackson or any other federal judge says it means—at least until they are reversed on appeal.

But what does it mean to a company that is supposed to obey this law? It means that there is no law, just a cloud of legal uncertainties, from which lightning can strike at any time.

In economics, "monopoly" means simply one seller. If you could invoke this provision of the Sherman Act only when there was just one seller, lots of Justice Department lawyers would be out of work, because there are very few products sold by only one company.

The ploy that prevents unemployment among anti-trust lawyers is to claim that some company sells a high percentage of some product—or, in the rhetoric of anti-trust, "controls" a large share of the market. And the way to produce statistics showing large shares is to define the market as narrowly as possible.

Judge Jackson does this by defining the market for operating systems like Microsoft's Windows as being only those operating systems using Intel's processors and their clones. That means we don't count Apple computers or computer systems relying on the Linux computer language.

These kinds of definitional games have been played throughout the history of anti-trust "law." The net result is that there are statistics showing many more "dominant" companies with "market power" in these narrowly defined industries than there would be if industries were defined in some economically meaningful way. Judge Jackson's pronouncements are larded with such ominous rhetoric.

What also runs through Judge Jackson's statements—and through the whole anti-trust tradition—is a confusion between competitors and competition. Harm to Microsoft's competitors is equated with harm to competition in the software industry. But nothing harms particular competitors like competition.

When Microsoft spent $100 million to develop its Internet browser and included it in Windows free of charge, to Judge Jackson that showed monopoly power and hurt competition. But why would a monopoly have to blow $100 million to improve its product?

It was precisely because Microsoft was not as optimistic as Judge Jackson about a lack of competition that they spent the money to keep their customers. Is it a violation of law to operate on a different economic theory than the one a judge believes in?

But suppose, for the sake of argument, that Microsoft was guilty of every terrible thing the Judge came up with. All the contract provisions he doesn't like can be forbidden and all the competitors who were supposed to have been harmed can be compensated to the tune of millions of dollars.

Why then is the Justice Department involved? Because they want the power to oversee and second-guess the computer software industry. Microsoft's competitors in Silicon Valley may rejoice at its legal misfortunes, but once Washington bureaucrats start calling the shots in the computer industry, their joy may be very short-lived. Silicon Valley rivals of Microsoft could turn out to be like those Democrats of a few years ago, who voted for special prosecutors as if they were only going to prosecute Republicans.

LESSONS
NOT
LEARNED

With all our looking back at the 20th century, we have missed some of its most blatant and most horrifying lessons. The worst horrors of that century, under both the Nazis and the Communists, came from concentrations of political power, brought about by heady rhetoric, powerful visions and emotional manipulations. Yet we remain as susceptible to all these things as if none of these horrors had happened.

The constitutional barriers that stand between us and the tyrannies that have swept over other peoples around the world are treated as things to be brushed aside or finessed when those who are skilled with words manipulate our emotions.

The constitution's proclamation of "equal protection of the laws" for all Americans is swept aside by saying the magic word "diversity," while creating preferences and quotas for some at the expense of others. Cry "Big Tobacco!" and due process of law vanishes into thin air. The first amendment to the constitution says that the right of free speech cannot even be infringed, but that is all forgotten in the stampede for "campaign finance reform."

There is nothing wrong with changing the constitution, which itself prescribes procedures for doing so. But we are playing with fire when we simply ignore the constitution or find clever ways around it. Without a constitution, we are at the mercy of whatever phrase or fashion sweeps across the political landscape.

Even Supreme Court justices, who are supposed to be guardians of the constitution, have often treated it as a nuisance to be gotten around or, worse yet, as political cover for using their power to advance whatever ideas they personally want to impose on the country. The federal government has only the powers specifically granted to it in the constitution, but many judges feel free to grant it more power when they happen to agree with its policies.

In a recent decision, Justice David Souter upheld campaign contribution restrictions on grounds that big contributions create "the perception of impropriety." Where does the constitution give the federal government the power to stop anything that creates the perception of impropriety? If it did, then any of our freedoms could be abolished just by using this magic phrase. Indeed, this decision opens the door to such an erosion in the years ahead.

Particular bad policies are the least of the dangers created by playing fast and loose with the constitution. Lawless power is the far greater danger—and has been for centuries, though its worst horrors seem to have been reserved for the 20th century.

Yet our judges, politicians and the intelligentsia play with fire as if they had never seen the conflagrations.

The constitution is only the most visible part of a cultural heritage that has given us freedoms which hundreds of millions of others around the world do not have. But dismantling that heritage is something that is being done every day—whether in anger or in fun—in our schools and colleges across the country, by people who congratulate themselves on being agents of "change."

Traditions distilled from the experiences of many generations past are treated as just somebody else's opinion, while we have a right to our own opinion, even when we are not yet a decade old. Children are told to discover their own ways of doing mathematics or of using the English language. They are encouraged to respond emotionally, rather than to analyze logically, on issues ranging from the environment to homelessness. "Public service" assignments give them emotional experiences without either the knowledge or the mental discipline to see below the surface.

In short, we and our children are being trained to be sheep and to respond automatically to words that strike an emotional chord. We are being set up to be played for suckers by anyone who wants to take up where the totalitarian movements of the 20th century left off.

The very tactics of those totalitarian movements—intimidation, demonization, and disregard of all rules in favor of politically defined results—have become hallmarks of political correctness today. Some people think political correctness is just silly. But many people thought Hitler was just silly before he took power and demonstrated how tragically mistaken they were.

Probably most of the people who go along with the destructive and dangerous trends of our time are no worse than the "useful idiots" who made totalitarianism possible. But that is bad enough.

LAW
ON
TRIAL

Law itself is on trial in an Albany courtroom where four New York City policemen are accused of murder in the shooting death of Amadou Diallo, an African immigrant. For a shockingly large number of people, the fact that the cops are white and the man who was shot was black is all they need to know in order to take sides.

And taking sides is the issue for them, not finding the truth or dispensing justice. This approach has already been tried extensively throughout the South during the Jim Crow era. It took decades of struggle and sacrifice—including the sacrifice of lives—to break down that system of double-standard "justice." Now it has come back into fashion again, with a new color scheme.

The tragic facts of the Diallo shooting are pretty plain. Even before the police arrived on the scene, Amadou Diallo was—for whatever reason—stationed in a doorway at night and periodically looking both ways up and down the street. Another resident of the area, coming home from work, was struck by what this resident says seemed to him at the time to be "suspicious" behavior. The prosecuting attorney immediately objected to this word and the judge immediately ordered it stricken from the record.

When a police car with four cops inside rolled by later,

after midnight, they too considered Diallo's behavior suspicious. When they stopped the car and got out, Diallo fled back inside the building. There, in a dimly lit hallway, he reached inside his jacket and pulled out a black object and held it out toward the cops. One of the policemen yelled "Gun!" By a horrible coincidence, another policeman toppled backwards off the steps onto the sidewalk, as if he had been shot, and his fellow officers opened fire on Diallo.

The driver of the car rushed toward the fallen officer and asked where he had been hit. But he had not been hit. He had just lost his balance and fallen back off the steps. Nor did Diallo have a gun. He had taken out his wallet and held it out toward the police. It was a tragedy of errors.

Enter the race hustlers, the politically correct media and politicians in an election year. Al Sharpton, who first gained fame by making wild accusations against policemen in the Tawana Brawley hoax, has of course jumped in with both feet and mobs of supporters. Hillary Clinton has called it "murder"—and she is a lawyer who should know better, especially with a trial going on.

Even in the courtroom, the atmosphere of intimidation has continued, unchecked by the judge who considered it offensive when a witness said that he found Diallo's actions suspicious.

Witnesses who have anything to say that might support the policemen's testimony have had wholly unnecessary identifying information publicized and read into the record. The witness who said that his suspicions caused him to pay attention to Diallo as he walked home after parking his truck not only had his address, but his apartment number as well, identified by the prosecutor in open court.

Supposedly this was to show that he lived in the rear and could not have seen what happened after he got home. But the witness had never claimed to have seen anything from his apartment. What this uncalled-for statement did was put the witness on notice in the courtroom that local neighborhood hotheads now knew where to find him and his family. It was a shot across his bow, a warning not only to him, but to any other witness who might say anything that would support what the policemen had said.

Do we wonder why witnesses don't come forward?

A nurse who heard the shots while attending a patient across the street was asked for the name of her patient, even though the patient was not a witness and never claimed to have seen or heard anything. When that was objected to, she was then asked whether the patient was male or female and how old. This was unconscionable in the atmosphere of hostility and lawlessness that has been whipped up over this shooting.

As someone who taught pistol shooting in the Marine Corps, I was not the least bit surprised by the number of shots fired—or by the fact that most of them missed. Nobody counts his own shots, much less other people's shots, in a life-and-death situation. This is not an arcade game, where lights go off to tell you whether you hit the target. You shoot until it looks safe to stop.

A lot of lights ought to go off about this trial and the way both witnesses and justice itself are being threatened, inside and outside the courtroom.

ABORTED
KNOWLEDGE

A certain professor who teaches students who aspire to become speech pathologists begins by showing them the development of the various organs involved in speech. When he shows his class an ultrasound picture of the development of the palate in an unborn baby, it is not uncommon for one or two women in his class to have tears in their eyes, or to say to him afterward that they have had an abortion and were very much affected by seeing what an unborn baby looks like.

For too long we have been led to believe that an abortion is the removal of some unformed material, something like having an appendix operation. The very expression "unborn baby" has almost disappeared from the language, being replaced by the more bloodless and antiseptic term "fetus."

Many vocal advocates who declare themselves "pro-choice" do not want women to have the choice of knowing just what they are choosing before having an abortion. Ferocious opposition has stopped the showing of pictures of an abortion in process—even in schools or colleges that show movies of naked adults performing various sex acts. Still photographs of aborted fetuses have been banned as well.

The particularly grisly procedure known as "partial-birth abortion" cannot even be referred to in much of the media, where it is called a "late-term abortion"—another bloodless term and one that shifts the focus from what happens to when it happens.

What happens in a partial-birth abortion is that a baby who has developed too far to die naturally when removed from his mother's body is deliberately killed by having his brains sucked out. When this is done, the baby is not completely out of his mother's body because, if he were, the doctor would be charged with murder. There is no medical reason for this procedure, which has been condemned by the American Medical Association. There is only a legal reason—to keep the doctor and the mother out of jail.

All this is smoothly covered over in the media by calling such actions a "late-term abortion" and refusing to specify what happens. Such patterns of determined evasions and obfuscations show that "pro-choice" in practice often really means pro-abortion. Knowledge is the first thing being aborted.

Philosophical questions about when life begins may preoccupy some people on both sides of the abortion controversy. But the raw physical facts of what happens in various kinds of abortion have turned many others, including physicians, from being pro-abortion to being anti-abortion. One doctor who had performed many abortions never performed another one after seeing an ultrasound movie of the baby's reactions.

With most other medical procedures, "informed consent" is the watchword. But, when the issue is abortion, great efforts are made to keep "choice" from becoming too informed.

Politically and legally, the abortion issue is too complex for any easy resolution. We have gone through a quarter of a century of bitter controversy precisely because the Supreme Court went for an easy resolution back in 1973 with the *Roe v. Wade* decision.

Before then, various states had made differing efforts to wrestle with and balance the weighty concerns on both sides of the abortion issue. But Supreme Court Justice Harry Blackmun rushed in where angels fear to tread, with a one-size-fits-all decision, washed down with the blatant lie that this was based on the Constitution.

Far from settling things, *Roe v. Wade* has led to polarization and escalating strife all across the country, including bombings and assassinations. It has corrupted the media, academia and other sources that are supposed to inform us, but which have instead become partisan organs of political correctness.

However this highly-charged issue is ultimately resolved—and there is no resolution on the horizon today—surely honesty must be part of that resolution. Political catch-phrases like "a woman's right to do what she wants with her own body" cannot be applied to situations where a baby is killed at the very moment when he ceases to be part of his mother's body.

One of the few signs of hope for some ultimate resolution is that most people on both sides of this controversy are not happy about abortions. The women who shed tears at the very sight of an unborn baby may not be politically committed to either side of this issue, but their feelings may be part of what is needed to bring opposing sides together.

MURDER
IS
MURDER

Everyone should be outraged by the murder of Matthew Sheppard—not because he was gay, but because he was a human being. We can only hope that the murderers' lawyers don't find a shrink who will say that "homophobia" is a disease and try to use that to get reduced sentences.

Already there are attempts to politicize this young man's murder by seeking laws against "hate crimes" and other items on the homosexual lobby's political agenda. In an era when so many people are so easily stampeded by words, we need to step back and think about what we are saying when we talk about "hate crimes." If Matthew Sheppard was not gay and was murdered for his insurance, would that make it any less of a crime?

People who glibly talk about "hate crimes" ignore both the past and the implications for the future in what they are advocating. It took centuries of struggle and people putting their lives on the line to get rid of the idea that a crime against "A" should be treated differently than the same crime committed against "B."

After much sacrifice and bloodshed, the principle finally prevailed that killing a peasant deserved the same punishment as killing a baron. Now the "hate crime" advocates want to undo all that and take us back to the days when punishment did not fit the crime, but varied with who the crime was committed against.

In the olden days, at least the law could readily apply its standard, even if it was a bad standard, because everyone could tell a peasant from a baron. But, once we make the punishment depend on motivation, we have entered never-never land, where opposing shrinks tell opposing stories to bewildered jurors, taking up lots of time in already overcrowded courts.

People who automatically respond to any problem by saying, "There ought to be a law" never seem to consider whether they are spreading existing law enforcement resources thinner and thinner. When new laws are passed, there is seldom even a consideration of whether to hire more police and more judges, much less build more courtrooms and more prisons.

Apparently it is OK just to spread the existing resources thinner. That makes sense only if the purpose of laws is to make people feel that they have "made a statement"—regardless of what the actual consequences may turn out to be.

Even more disturbing than such irresponsible uses of the law is the notion that there should be "gay rights," "women's rights" and various ethnic group "rights." The Fourteenth Amendment provides for equal rights and equal protection of the laws. If you want more than that, then you are no longer talking about rights, but about special privileges.

Unfortunately, the rhetoric of victimhood has been used repeatedly over the past few decades to claim special privileges—and not just by homosexuals. The time is long overdue for everyone to wake up and not let this game go on forever—or until it has us all at each others' throats.

Special privileges are poisonous to a whole society. Often those who claim these privileges become victims of the backlash.

Even when the privileges are not put into the law but consist only of special indulgences for rotten behavior that would not be tolerated by other members of the society, this too is poisonous in itself, as well as breeding inevitable backlashes.

Many of those who are loudest in their demands for "gay rights" and in breast-beating over their "identity" show the least respect for other people's rights and even go out of their way to insult Catholics or others who do not share their lifestyle. Homosexuals do not need my approval, but neither do they have a right to my approval—or to propagandize a captive audience of children in the public schools to get their approval or to acquire new recruits.

Homosexuals are not unique in trying to cash in victimhood for privileges, if only the privilege of insulting other people with impunity. But neither they nor anyone else should be allowed to get away with this.

It is not at all clear that most homosexuals go along with the goals and tactics of those who proclaim themselves their "leaders." When you consider how many other groups' "leaders" advocate things to which most members of those groups are opposed, there is little basis for taking "gay rights" advocates at their word, much less let what they say be the last word for the whole society.

McVEIGH
AND THE
DEATH PENALTY

The execution of Timothy McVeigh has again raised the issue of capital punishment. Much of the case against capital punishment does not rise above the level of opaque pronouncements that it is "barbaric," by which those who say this presumably mean that it makes them unhappy to think of killing another human being. It should. But we do many things that we don't like to do because the alternative is to have things that make us even more unhappy.

As Adam Smith said, two centuries ago, "Mercy to the guilty is cruelty to the innocent." Those who lost loved ones in the Oklahoma City bombing do not need to spend the rest of their lives having their deep emotional wounds rubbed raw, again and again, by seeing Timothy McVeigh and his lawyers spouting off in the media. McVeigh inflicted more than enough cruelty on them already and they need to begin to heal.

Sometimes those who oppose capital punishment talk about "the sanctity of human life." Ironically, many of these same people have no such reluctance to kill innocent unborn babies as they have to execute a mass murderer. But the issue of capital punishment comes up only because the murderer has already violated the sanctity of human life. Are we to say that his life has more sanctity than the life or lives he has taken?

Shabby logic often tries to equate the murderer's act of taking a life with the law's later taking of his life. But physical parallels are not moral parallels. Otherwise, after a bank robber seizes money at gunpoint, the police would be just as wrong to take the money back from him at gunpoint. A woman who used force to fight off a would-be rapist would be just as guilty as he was for using force against her.

It is a sign of how desperate the opponents of capital punishment are that they have to resort to such "reasoning." Since these are not all stupid people, by any means, it is very doubtful if these are the real reasons for their opposition to executions. A writer for the liberal *New Republic* magazine may have been closer to the reason when he painfully spoke on TV about how terrible he felt to watch someone close to him die.

Nothing is more universal than the pain of having someone dear to you die, whether or not you witness it. Nor should anyone rejoice at inflicting such pain on someone else. But one of the fatal weaknesses of the political left is its unwillingness to weigh one thing against another. Criminals are not executed for the fun of it. They are executed to deter them from repeating their crime, among other reasons.

Squeamishness is not higher morality, even though the crusade against capital punishment attracts many who cannot resist anything that allows them to feel morally one-up on others.

It is dogma on the political left that capital punishment does not deter. But it is indisputable that execution deters the murderer who is executed. Nor is this any less significant because it is obvious. There are people who would be alive today if the convicted murderers who killed them had been executed for their previous murders.

Glib phrases about instead having "life in prison without the possibility of parole" are just talk. Murderers kill again in prison. They escape from prison and kill. They are furloughed and kill while on furlough. And there is no such thing as life in prison without the possibility of a liberal governor coming along to pardon them or commute their sentence. That too has happened.

The great fear of people on both sides of the capital punishment debate is making an irretrievable mistake by executing an innocent person. Even the best legal system cannot eliminate human error 100%. If there were an option that would prevent any innocent person from dying as a result of our legal system, that option should be taken. But there is no such option.

Letting murderers live has cost, and will continue to cost, the lives of innocent people. The only real question is whether more innocent lives will be lost this way than by executing the murderers, even with the rare mistake—which we should make as rare as possible—of executing an innocent person.

As so often in life, there is no real "solution" with a happy ending. There is only a trade-off. Those who cannot bring themselves to face trade-offs in general are of course unable to face this most painful of all trade-offs. But they have no right to consider their hand-wringing as higher morality. People are being murdered while they are wringing their hands.

PART VI
SOCIAL ISSUES

BOOMERS
AND
BOOMERANGS

Time was when grandparents often moved in with their children and grandchildren, especially when the grandparent was a widow or widower, or just had trouble making ends meet financially. Today, it is the children and grandchildren who move in with the grandparents.

A recent Census Bureau report shows that there are three times as many households where the children and grandchildren are living in the grandparents' home as there are where the grandparents are living with their children and grandchildren. Moreover, this trend is growing.

Back in 1970, there were a little more than 2 million children under 18 who were living in their grandparents' households. By 1997, that had reached nearly 4 million. Six percent of all children under 18 live in their grandparents' households.

There was a time when any adult who had gone out into the world would be embarrassed to come back and live with his parents, much less bring his or her family too. Today, this is such a common occurrence among the baby boomers that there is a word for grown children who leave home and then come back—"boomerangs."

Perhaps the worst situation of all is when both parents have skipped out and dumped their children on grandma and grandpa. This happens about one-third of the time when grandchildren are living in their grandparents' home.

These grandparents are not rich people living on investments and annuities. Most of the grandparents are working, even if their children aren't. Moreover, they suffer more depression and other health problems than grandparents without such burdens.

Bad as this is, what is worse is to contemplate what is going to happen when the last of the responsible generation—those who feel a responsibility to look out for both their aging parents and their adult children—pass from the scene, leaving behind only the "me" generation.

This is only one of many social time bombs ticking away, while we enjoy a prospering economy. We may hope that the "me" generation will grow up when they run out of other people to dump their responsibilities on. But don't bet the rent money on it.

People don't usually grow up when there are other people who make excuses for their immaturity. In a "non-judgmental" world, who is to tell irresponsible parents to grow up?

Even when the parents are present and have their children in their own homes, they seem increasingly to be letting these children pretty much raise themselves. When a woman was complaining recently about some bratty and even dangerous behavior she sees in children, I asked, "Where are their parents?" She replied: "There are no parents today." I had to admit that she had a point.

One of the biggest excuses for lax parenting is that both parents "have to" work, in order to "make ends meet." Yet, within living memory, it was common in working-class families—black and white—for the husband to work and the wife to stay home to raise the children. Why didn't both parents have to work then, in order to make ends meet?

Were people so much richer then? On the contrary, they were much poorer. Today's families living in poverty have things that average Americans could not afford then.

People today eat in restaurants more times in a month than they used to in a year—or, in some cases, a decade. As a young man, I was uneasy when I began eating in restaurants, because I had so seldom eaten in one while growing up. As for having a car, the thought never crossed my mind.

If people in those days had lived the way we live today, of course it would have taken both parents working to make ends meet. They would probably have had to put the children to work too.

People make choices and have their own priorities—and adults take responsibilities for their choices and priorities. It is a cop-out to say that they are "forced" to have two-income families just "to make ends meet."

When we have a system where children are fed in schools and other basic responsibilities are also lifted from the shoulders of their parents, why should we be surprised that the sense of parental responsibility seems to be eroding? We are not surprised when a couch potato doesn't have the kind of muscles found on someone who exercises. Our society is increasingly turning out moral couch potatoes.

DEEP TROUBLE
FROM
SHALLOW PEOPLE

A recent news story told of an Asian-American girl applying to Wesleyan University with test scores in the 1400s and a Dominican girl applying to the same institution with test scores in the 900s. A member of the admissions committee recommended against admitting the Asian-American girl and in favor of admitting the Dominican girl.

Why? The Dominican girl had more handicaps to overcome. Besides, the admissions committee member added, "I am willing to take a chance on her."

Actually, he is taking no chance whatever. He will not lose one dime if this girl fails miserably. The people who will lose will be the people who have contributed their money to Wesleyan University, in order to promote education, and instead have their contributions used to make some admissions committee member feel like a little tin god.

The Dominican girl herself will also lose if she goes in unprepared and fails, when she could have gotten some additional preparation first and then applied to a less demanding college, where she would have a better chance of success. Above all, American society loses when such feel-good self-indulgences undermine the connection between performance and reward, reducing incentives for high-ability, low-ability, and average students alike.

Unfortunately, this admissions committee member is by no means unique. All across the country, at both elite institutions and non-elite institutions, admissions committee members act as if they have some deep insight which enables them to judge individuals' inner motivations, rather than their actual record—and to pick out those who will become "leaders," as that undefined term is conceived in the psychobabble of the day.

This would be incredible arrogance, even if admissions committees were composed of higher-caliber people than they usually are. Given the kinds of third-raters who too often find their way onto admissions committees, even at elite colleges, it is a tragic farce. After all, someone who has graduated from Harvard or MIT with top honors is likely to have a lot better career options than becoming a staffer on an admissions committee at Harvard or MIT.

The mystery is not why shallow people do shallow things. The mystery is why we put so much arbitrary power in the hands of shallow people—especially when that power would be dangerous in anybody's hands. College admissions committees are just one example.

Social workers have gotten gestapo-like powers to snatch people's children from their homes on the basis of unsubstantiated charges that have never even been heard in a court of law. They can deny an orphan a decent home because the family that wants to adopt does not fit their arbitrary notions and unproven theories. Minority children have especially been denied homes with white families who want them and instead have been consigned to a life of drifting from one foster home to another for years on end.

Our public schools are the most massive examples of arbitrary power put into the hands of shallow people. While social work and college admissions committees usually fail to attract people of high intelligence, the public schools positively repel many such people by requiring them to sit through years of unbelievably stupid education courses, as a precondition for a permanent career.

Students' whole futures depend on getting a decent education, but their teachers may prefer using them as guinea pigs for the latest fads, such as psychological manipulation, social engineering and proselytizing for politically correct causes. If—heaven help us—the child is very bright and is bored to death by the drivel presented by shallow teachers, the answer may well be to drug the student with Ritalin, rather than let him or her become restless.

The time is long overdue for us all to recognize that there are tasks and roles beyond the capacity of even the most intelligent people—and that only the least intelligent are likely to take on those impossible roles. It has been known for centuries that fools rush in where angels fear to tread.

There is no need to abolish college admissions committees, social workers or teachers. But their roles need to be kept within much narrower and more defined bounds. Above all, what they do must be subjected to some test other than what makes them feel good or what sounds good to their like-minded colleagues. Otherwise, we are putting the inmates in charge of the asylum.

THANKSGIVING
AND
"FAIRNESS"

There was a time when Thanksgiving meant an occasion for counting our blessings. But, now that we have so many blessings that previous generations could hardly have dreamed about, we take them all for granted and are much more likely to count our grievances and the ways in which others have been unfair to us.

Everybody is for "fairness"—because we all use the same word to mean very different things. Most of us think you have been treated fairly when you have been treated the same as everyone else—subjected to the same rules and judged by the same standards. But some think that you have been treated fairly only if you have had the same chances as everyone else.

These are very different and completely incompatible notions. When the rules of basketball treat me the same as they treat Michael Jordan, that does not mean that we have equal chances of success. In fact, that virtually guarantees that I have no chance.

People on opposite sides of political and legal issues often talk right past each other because they are using the same words to mean totally different and mutually contradictory things. When statistics are flung around on the "disparities"— often called "inequities"—between different groups, the implication is that such statistical differences could not exist without unfair treatment.

Even in situations where there is a total absence of evidence for this unfair treatment, that scarcely causes a pause. If there is no evidence, then there must be "covert" discrimination, a "glass ceiling" or some other elusive and sinister influence that you cannot substantiate. This kind of circular reasoning says in effect, "heads I win and tails you lose."

Politically, there are few ideas more potent than the notion that all your problems are caused by other people and their unfairness to you. That notion was the royal road to unbridled power for Hitler, Lenin, Mao, and Pol Pot—which is to say, millions of human beings paid with their lives for believing it.

The unfairness that these demagogues talked about was not a myth. Nothing is easier than finding examples of unfair treatment among human beings. The fatal misstep is in assuming that such unfairness can be presumed whenever results are unequal. For the truly clever, unfairness is simply defined as anything producing unequal results or unequal prospects.

To those with this mindset, if individuals' "life chances" are unequal, then that is unfair. This might be an interesting argument if you were filing a class action lawsuit against God, but it is idiocy when trying to hold any given human being responsible for a whole galaxy of complex interactions beyond the control of anyone made of flesh and blood.

When we confuse the vagaries of fate with the sins of man and look for "leaders" to redress this unfairness, we are setting ourselves up to become dupes of those who know how to arouse emotions and promise the impossible. That lesson is written in blood across the history of the 20th century.

Any serious study of geography alone would show the utter unrealism of expecting people whose histories and cultures evolved in very different physical settings to have the same skills and experiences. How could the peoples living in the Himalayas have developed the same seafaring skills as people living in the Greek islands? How could the Eskimos have learned to grow pineapples?

These are just some of the more obvious geographic sources of unequal results—and geography is just one of many influences on our ability to create wealth or do the thousands of other things which influence our "life chances." First-born children average higher IQs than later children. Technology makes some people's jobs obsolete and opens up great opportunities for others.

The unfairness of other people is just one more item on this very long list. How many are interested in the unfairness that has made us so much more fortunate than people in previous centuries? If the average American of today could be transported back over the centuries and become a nobleman in the Middle Ages, that would produce a reduced standard of living and a shorter life span. Maybe that is a reason to count our blessings instead of our grievances.

WAS
THE BALL
JUICED?

When Mark McGwire had his incredible 70-home run season in 1998, nobody thought that his record would be broken just three years later. Babe Ruth's record of 60 home runs lasted 34 years, until Roger Maris broke it by one home run in 1961 and then held the record for another 37 years. But Maris' mark has been topped six times within the past three years by Mark McGwire, Sammy Sosa and Barry Bonds.

Spectacular increases in home runs have often raised the question: Has the ball been juiced up to travel farther, in order to increase the number of home runs? That question was raised back in 1961, when Roger Maris hit 61 home runs, and it was raised even earlier when Babe Ruth first ushered in the era of big home run hitters in the 1920s. For a long time, the period before 1920 has been referred to as the "dead ball" era and the period after 1920 as the "lively ball" era.

There was stronger statistical evidence of a sea-change in home run hitting before and after 1920 than in more recent times. From 1900 to 1920, only three batters hit 20 or more home runs in a season and none hit 30. Moreover, each of these three batters did it only once during that era. But, during the 1920s, half a dozen players hit 40 or more home runs in a season, with Babe Ruth doing it eight times.

This dramatic change in home run production in both major leagues was long regarded as proof positive that the ball had been changed. But a closer look suggests that it was batting styles that changed. It was not the existing sluggers who suddenly started hitting many more home runs. It was the new sluggers, with new batting styles, who began hitting unprecedented numbers of home runs in the 1920s.

None of the established batting stars of the years before 1920—Ty Cobb, Tris Speaker, Joe Jackson, Eddie Collins—hit as many as 20 home runs in a season during the decade of the 1920s. Some of the old-timers had big seasons in the 1920s, but that did not include big home run totals.

Eddie Collins topped .330 five times during that decade but never broke into double digits in home runs. Ty Cobb and Tris Speaker, between them, hit over .350 seven times during the 1920s, but Speaker's highest home run total was 17 and Cobb never exceeded 12. Neither did Shoeless Joe Jackson. And they were all hitting the same ball that Babe Ruth was hitting.

The top hitters of the past continued to hit as they always had—choked up on the bat and going for contact, rather than swinging for the fences. It was the new players, who grabbed the bat down at the end of the handle like Ruth, who began hitting the ball out of the park with greater frequency.

Those who hit 40 or more home runs during the 1920s either began their careers in that decade (Lou Gehrig, Mel Ott, Chuck Klein) or reached their peak then (Babe Ruth, Rogers Hornsby, Cy Williams). If it was the ball that was responsible for the big surge in home runs, then the old and the new batting stars alike would have seen dramatic increases in homers. But that was not what happened.

When Roger Maris broke Ruth's home run record in 1961, it was during the first year of baseball's expansion beyond the 16-team limit that had existed since the beginning of the century. With expansion teams stretching the pitching thin, many batters had banner years. But the three top pitchers all had earned run averages under 3.00 in 1961, while throwing the same ball as the rookie pitchers who were rushed into the big leagues and the washed-up pitchers who were able to hang on with expansion teams.

The most recent escalation of home run hitting has come at a time of bigger players and smaller ball parks. Not only have the new stadiums been built with shorter distances to the fences, older parks like Yankee Stadium have been remodeled to bring the fences closer. It used to be 415 feet to the left field bullpen in Yankee Stadium, but it is not that far to dead center field in most of the major league parks today. None has the 461 feet to the center field wall that Yankee Stadium had during the careers of Ruth, Gehrig, DiMaggio and Mantle.

You can never prove a negative, so those who want to believe that the ball has been juiced can continue to believe that. But the evidence is against them.

THE DANGERS
OF
"EQUALITY"

Any smell more subtle than ammonia or a sewage treatment plant is usually hard for me to detect. However, I happen to be able to smell gas escaping better than most people. On more than one occasion I have walked by someone's home, smelled gas and left a note on the door. While later passing that house again, I have seen the gas company out digging up the ground, and—after that—no more smell of gas.

A sense of smell is just one of innumerable things that can differ greatly from one person to the next. Moreover, many of these differences are essential to the survival and progress of the human race.

People have different vulnerabilities and resistances to a variety of diseases. That is why one disease is unlikely to wipe out the human species, even in one place. An epidemic that sweeps through an area may leave some people dying like flies while others remain as healthy as horses.

There are children who are years late in beginning to talk and yet who end up scoring over the 90th percentile on math tests. Then there are other children whose speech is so precocious that they sound like little geniuses when you hear them talk—and yet they have trouble subtracting two from four or tying their own shoelaces—and always will.

Individuals differ radically from one another in all sorts of skills, interests and talents. What all this means is that the capabilities of the human race vastly exceed the capabilities of even the brightest and the best individuals.

When the brightest and the best take over making decisions for other people, usually through the power of government, those decisions are likely to be based on less knowledge, experience and understanding than when ordinary people make their own individual decisions for themselves. The anointed may know more than the average person, but far less than all the ordinary people put together.

Scientists who study the brain say that some abilities develop greatly at the expense of other abilities. Socially as well, some talents are developed by neglecting others. Concert pianists seldom have a college education, because the demands of the two things are just too great. Therefore, for both biological and social reasons, the only way for everyone to be equal would be for them to be equal at a lower level of ability than what some people are capable of in some things and other people are in other things.

In other words, if everyone were equal in their many capabilities, the whole species would be no more capable or insightful or resistant to diseases than one individual. Our chances of surviving or progressing would be a lot less than they are now. Even the enjoyment we get from watching Tiger Woods play golf or Pavarotti sing would be lost, for we would all be mediocrities in golf and singing and a thousand other things.

A recent book on the publishing industry showed that 63 out of 100 best-sellers had been written by just six authors. It is not uncommon in baseball for just two players to hit more than half the home runs hit by the whole team.

Ironically, the fact that nearly two-thirds of the best-sellers were written by the likes of Tom Clancy and Danielle Steel was revealed by a man who was one of the founders of the left-wing *New York Review of Books*. Yet one of the key assumptions of the left is that statistical disparities are suspicious, if not sinister, especially if these are differences in income and wealth.

But if people differ radically in performance, why is it surprising that they also differ radically in the rewards they receive? And if we are determined to equalize, can we equalize upward or only downward? Can you make a mediocre golfer another Tiger Woods or only penalize Tiger Woods for being better?

Where the desire for equality turns from a quixotic hope to a dangerous gamble is in politics. To create even the semblance of equality requires a concentration of power in the hands of political leaders. And, as the history of the 20th century has shown repeatedly and tragically, in countries around the world, once concentrated power is put into the hands of political leaders, they can use it for whatever purpose they have in mind—regardless of what others had in mind when they granted them that power.

Becoming the pawns of politicians is a high price to pay for letting demagogues stir up our envy and beguile us with promises to equalize.

IS
THE FAMILY
BECOMING EXTINCT?

To the intelligentsia, the family—or "the traditional family," as they say nowadays—is just one lifestyle among many. Moreover, they periodically announce its decline, with no sign whatever of regret. Sometimes with just a touch of smugness.

The latest census data show that the traditional family—a married couple and their children—constitutes just a little less than one-fourth of all households. On the other hand, such families constituted just a little more than one-fourth of all families a decade ago. Any reports of the demise of the traditional family are greatly exaggerated.

Snapshot statistics can be very misleading when you realize that people go through different stages of their lives. Even the most traditional families—including Ozzie and Harriet themselves—never permanently consisted of married couples and their children. Kids grow up and move out. People who get married do not start having children immediately. If every single person in the country got married and had children, married-couple families with children would still not constitute 100 percent of households at any given time.

With rising per-capita incomes, more individuals can afford to have their own households. These include young unmarried adults, widows and widowers, and others who often lived with relatives in earlier times. When more such households are created, traditional family households automatically become a smaller percentage of all households.

Incidentally, the growth of households containing one person—about 25 percent of all households today—is the reason why average household incomes are rising very little, even though per capita incomes have been rising very substantially. Gloom and doomers love to cite household income statistics, in order to claim that Americans' incomes are stagnating, when in fact there has been an unprecedented and sustained rise in prosperity, among women and men, blacks and whites, and virtually everybody else.

Marriage does occur later today than in the past and more people don't get married at all. But 53 percent of all households still contain married couples, with or without children currently living with them, while some of the other households contain widows and widowers whose marriages were ended only by death.

Despite attempts to equate married couples with people who are living together as "domestic partners," married couples are in fact better off than people who are not married, by almost any standard you can think of. Married couples have higher incomes, longer lives, better health, less violence, less alcohol and less poverty.

As Casey Stengel used to say, "You can look it up." One place to look it up is in the book *The Case for Marriage* by Linda Waite and Maggie Gallagher. But this is just one place among many. You don't usually hear these kinds of facts because they are not considered to be "politically correct" when the media, politicians, academia and the courts are busy trying to make all kinds of living arrangements seem equal.

The latest census report on "America's Families and Living Arrangements" contains all sorts of statistics but avoids showing the most basic statistics on the average income of married-couple families compared with "other family households" or with "non-family households." The Census Bureau apparently does not want to be politically incorrect.

If you dig through the census' numbers, however, you will discover some revealing clues. While both "unmarried partners" and "married spouses" are spread up and down the income scale, the bracket with the largest number of men who are unmarried partners is the bracket between $30,000 and $40,000. The bracket with the largest number of husbands is between $50,000 and $75,000. Among married-couple households, the bracket with the largest number of households is $75,000 and over. Among "other family groups," the bracket with the largest number of households is that under $10,000.

Women who are shacking up are four times as likely as wives to become victims of violence, and their children are 40 times as likely to be abused by live-in boy friends as by their own parents.

Despite all this, it remains dogma among those who set the ideological fashions that marriage is just another lifestyle, no better or worse than any other. Even the Census Bureau seems unwilling to publish statistical data that would go against this vision and rile up the anointed.

LIFE
AT THE
BOTTOM

Poverty used to mean hunger and inadequate clothing to protect you against the elements, as well as long hours of grinding labor to try to make ends meet. But today most of the people living below the official poverty line not only have enough food, they are actually slightly more likely than others to be overweight. Ordinary clothing is so plentiful that young hoodlums fight over designer clothes or fancy sneakers. As for work, there is less of that in lower income households today than among the affluent.

Most of today's poor have color TV and microwave ovens. Poverty in the old physical sense is nowhere near as widespread as it once was. Yet life at the bottom is no picnic—and is too often a nightmare.

A recently published book titled *Life at the Bottom* paints a brilliantly insightful, but very painful, picture of the underclass—its emptiness, agonies, violence and moral squalor. This book is about a British underclass neighborhood where its author, Theodore Dalrymple, works as a doctor. That may in fact make its message easier for many Americans to understand and accept.

Most of the people that Dalrymple writes about are white, so it may be possible at last to take an honest look at the causes and consequences of an underclass lifestyle, without fear of

being called "racist." The people who are doing the same socially destructive and self-destructive things that are being
done in underclass neighborhoods in the United States cannot
claim that it is because their ancestors were enslaved or because they face racial discrimination.

Once those cop-outs are out of the way, maybe we can face
reality and even talk sense about how things became such a
mess and such a horror. As an emergency room physician,
Theodore Dalrymple treats youngsters who have been beaten
up so badly that they require medical attention—because they
tried to do well in school. When that happens in American
ghettos, the victims have been accused of "acting white" by
trying to get an education. On the other side of the Atlantic,
both the victims and the hoodlums are white.

The British underclass neighborhood in which Dalrymple
works, like its American counterpart, features what he calls
"the kind of ferocious young egotist to whom I would give a
wide berth in the broadest daylight." He sees also "the destruction of the strong family ties that alone made emergence from
poverty possible for large numbers of people."

Dalrymple's own father was born in a slum—but in a very
different social setting from that of today's underclass. For one
thing, his father received a real education. The textbooks from
which he was taught would be considered too tough in today's
era of dumbed-down education.

Dalrymple's father was given the tools to rise out of poverty, while today's underclass is not only denied those tools,
but receives excuses for remaining in poverty—and ideologies
blaming their plight on others, whom they are encouraged to
envy and resent. The net result is an underclass generation
that has trouble spelling simple words or doing elementary
arithmetic, and which has no intention of developing job
skills.

By having their physical needs taken care of by the welfare state, as if they were livestock, the underclass are left with "a life emptied of meaning," as Dalrymple says, since they cannot even take pride in providing their own food and shelter, as generations before them did. Worse, they are left with no sense of responsibility in a non-judgmental world.

Some educators, intellectuals, and others may imagine that they are being friends of the poor by excusing or "understanding" their self-destructive behavior and encouraging a paranoid view of the larger world around them. But the most important thing anyone can do for the poor is to help them get out of poverty, as Dalrymple's father was helped by those who taught him and held him to standards—treating him as a responsible human being, not livestock.

No summary can do justice to the vivid examples and penetrating insights in *Life at the Bottom*. It needs to be read—with the understanding that its story is also our story.

GAY
MARRIAGE

The issue of gay marriage is one of many signs of the sloppy thinking of our times. Centuries of laws, policies and traditions have grown up around marriage as a union of a man and a woman. Now the demand is that all those laws, policies and traditions simply be transferred automatically and en masse to an entirely different union that chooses to use the same word.

Homosexuals were on their strongest ground when they argued that what happens between consenting adults is nobody else's business. Now they want to make it everybody's business by requiring others to acquiesce in their unions and treat them as they would other unions, both in law and in social practice.

Why is marriage a government concern in the first place? There are at least three reasons.

First of all, a marriage between a man and a woman has the potential to produce additional people, who are neither consenting nor adults. The wellbeing of these children is important both for their sake and for the sake of the society as a whole, whose future these children represent. This consideration obviously does not apply to homosexual unions.

Second, men and women are inherently in very different positions within a marriage. The inescapable fact that only women become pregnant means that male and female situations are never going to be the same, no matter how much "gender neutral" language we use or how much fashionable talk there is about how "we" are going to have a baby. Laws must make them jointly responsible for the baby that she alone will have. This consideration likewise does not apply to homosexual unions.

Third, time has very different effects on men and women. As the years pass and women lose their physical attraction, men are typically rising in income and occupational status. It is usually easier for a middle-aged man to abandon his wife and make a second marriage with a younger "trophy wife" than for a woman to remarry equally as advantageously. Since a woman has often invested years of her life in creating a home and family, the marriage contract is one way of trying to assure her that this investment will not be in vain.

These and other differences between the sexes simply do not apply when the people in a domestic union are of the same sex. When they are simply "consenting adults," they can consent on whatever terms they choose to work out between themselves. It is nobody else's business and should not be the law's business.

If they choose to consider themselves married, that is wholly different from saying that a whole elaborate body of laws, policies and traditions—which evolved from the experiences of innumerable generations of male and female unions—should automatically apply to their very different circumstances. You can call yourself anything you want, including the queen of Sheba, but that does not give you the right to force other people to call you the queen of Sheba.

After years of dumbed-down education, it may be inevitable that we would now have a population which includes many people who cannot see beyond words to the realities that those words are supposed to convey. It is hard to imagine any previous generation of Americans who would have taken seriously the idea of making marriage laws apply to domestic unions which lack the very features that caused marriage laws to exist in the first place.

The issue of gay marriage is just one of many examples of the victim's ploy, which says: "I am a victim. Therefore, if you do not give in to my demands and let me walk over you like a doormat, it shows that you are a hate-filled, evil person." Whatever its failings as logic, this tactic has been a big success politically.

The only rewards for giving in to unreasonable demands are more unreasonable demands. Having gotten far more money spent for AIDS than has been spent on other fatal diseases affecting far more people, gay activists are now demanding federal research on the kinds of recreational drugs used in night clubs by homosexuals, so as to make them safer. Imagine if alcoholics were to demand that the feds spend tax dollars to make drunkenness safer!

Homosexuals are not the only group to have played this game—and won. Our vulnerability to such ploys is far more dangerous than any particular issue or any particular group, because it means that we are sitting ducks for any slick political demagogues who come along and choose to take away anything we have, including our freedom and everything else that makes this America.

THE
EINSTEIN
SYNDROME

What have famed pianist Arthur Rubinstein, Italian dictator Benito Mussolini, India's self-taught mathematical genius Ramanujan, Nobel Prize-winning economist Gary Becker, talk show host G. Gordon Liddy and renowned physicists Richard Feynman, Edward Teller and Albert Einstein all had in common?

Aside from being remarkable people, they were all late in beginning to speak when they were children. Edward Teller, for example, did not say anything that anyone understood until he was four years old. Einstein began talking at age three but he was still not fluent when he turned nine.

While most children who are late in beginning to speak are male, there have also been some famous female late-talkers—celebrated 19th century pianist Clara Schumann and outstanding 20th century mathematician Julia Robinson, the first woman to become president of the American Mathematical Association. In addition, there have been innumerable people of exceptional ability in a number of fields who were years behind the norm for developing the ability to speak when they were children.

Parents and professionals alike have been baffled as to the reason for delayed speech in children whose precocious intellectual development has been obvious, even when they are toddlers. Some of these kids can put together puzzles designed for older children or for adults. Some can use computers by themselves as early as age two, even though they remain silent while their peers are developing the ability to speak.

No one really knows for sure why this is so. But these children have only begun to be studied within the past decade. My own book *The Einstein Syndrome* is one such study. More research on these children is being conducted by Professor Stephen Camarata at the Vanderbilt University medical school. He was himself late in talking.

Research on Einstein's brain has suggested to some neuroscientists that he was late in talking because of the unusual development of his brain, as revealed by an autopsy. Those portions of his brain where analytical thinking was concentrated had spread out far beyond their usual area and spilled over into adjoining areas, including the region from which speech is usually controlled. This has led some neuroscientists to suggest that his genius and his late talking could have been related.

At this point, no one knows whether this is the reason why Einstein took so long to develop the ability to speak, much less whether this is true of the other people of outstanding intellect who were also late in beginning to speak. What is known, however, is that there are a number of disabilities that are more common among people of high intellect than in the general population.

Members of the high-IQ Mensa society, for example, have a far higher than normal incidence of allergies. A sample of youngsters enrolled in the Johns Hopkins program for mathematically precocious youths—kids who can score 700 on the math SAT when they are just 12 years old—showed that more than four-fifths of them were allergic and/or myopic and/or left-handed.

This is all consistent with one region of the brain having above normal development and taking resources that leave some other region or regions with less than the usual resources for performing other functions. It is also consistent with the fact that some bright children who talk late remain impervious to all attempts of parents or professionals to get them to talk at the normal time. Yet these same kids later begin to speak on their own, sometimes after parents have finally just given up hope and stopped trying.

Noted language authority and neuroscientist Steven Pinker of MIT says, "language seems to develop about as quickly as the growing brain can handle it." While this was a statement about the general development of language, it may be especially relevant to bright children who talk late. As the whole brain grows in early childhood, increasing the total resources available, the regions whose resources have been preempted elsewhere can now catch up and develop normally.

My research and that of Professor Camarata have turned up a number of patterns in children with the Einstein Syndrome that were similar to what biographies of Einstein himself reveal. Most children who talk late are not like those in our studies. But a remarkable number are.

Unfortunately, many of these children get misdiagnosed as retarded, autistic or as having an attention deficit disorder.

LOOSE
LIPS

Some of the intelligentsia are yelling louder than ever that they are being silenced. Professors, journalists and others who have made grossly offensive remarks in the wake of the September 11th terrorist attack are shocked that other Americans are criticizing them for it. To them, apparently, free speech means being free of criticism by others who want to exercise their own free speech rights.

As the *Chronicle of Higher Education*—the trade publication of academia—put it, "professors across the country have found their freedom to speak hemmed in by incensed students, alumni, and university officials." Apparently none of these people has a right to be incensed or to express their reactions to the profs.

The self-righteousness of those who want to be exempt from criticism is incredible. According to the *Chronicle of Higher Education*, events "have left emotions so raw that people are struggling to think critically about what happened— and some administrators would prefer that professors not even try."

Thinking critically? When a professor at the University of New Mexico makes a joke approving the attack on the Pentagon, is that thinking critically—or thinking at all? At one of the California State University campuses, a professor who said that American actions had helped bring on the terrorist attacks was "shocked by the anger his remarks prompted."

Even the *Chronicle of Higher Education*, while characterizing these responses as "part of the American impulse toward anti-intellectualism," has to admit that "no one has been fired or locked up for joking about bombs or criticizing President Bush." All that has happened is that others have asserted their own rights of free speech. But even that is said to have a "chilling effect." As one professor at the University of Texas put it, the message from the academic administration was "if you stick your neck out, we will disown you."

Apparently other people don't even have a right to disassociate themselves from your remarks. Apparently anything short of uncritical acceptance of whatever asinine statements the profs make seems to them like a violation of the First Amendment.

This seeking of privileges in the name of rights extends far beyond the campuses. Journalists have been wrapping themselves in the First Amendment for years—even as they assume the role of citizens of the world, who soar above the parochial concerns of the United States of America. One of the cable networks doesn't want its employees to use the word "terrorists" to describe those who launched an attack that killed thousands of American civilians.

Various media outlets apparently feel a need to give equal time, if not moral equivalence, to Osama bin Laden and others in the terrorist organizations.

Would anyone have thought of giving Hitler free time to broadcast his propaganda on networks during World War II?

The most unconscionable media act of all may well have been the banner headline on the front of the *New York Times* of October 10, 2001: "U.S. Said to Plan Copter Raids in Afghanistan." The *Times'* motto is "All the News That's Fit to

Print." But, while reporting what has happened is news, reporting what is about to happen with American troops in a military operation is more like espionage.

Nor is this the first time that the media have been reckless with the lives of fellow Americans in combat. During the Gulf War a decade ago, one of the reporters on the scene broadcast to the world that the Iraqi missiles being fired at American troops were missing and landing "five miles north of here." That is the kind of information that an enemy needs to adjust his range. It is the kind of information which spies and spotters are supposed to provide. But here it was being supplied free of charge.

Perhaps that is what to expect from journalists who claim all the privileges of Americans, while acting as citizens of the world, neutral as between "both sides." Since they are so totally incapable of self-criticism, the rest of us should at least understand the implications of their self-indulgence.

There are American troops who can die needlessly in combat, and American children who can grow up as orphans, because somebody forgot the old wartime maxim, "Loose lips sink ships." There is great consternation in the press and in Congress that President Bush has ordered stricter limits on who gets military briefings. But it is reassuring that irresponsible people will now have adult supervision.

"THE DUTY
TO
DIE"

Our betters have been telling us how to live our lives for so long that it is only the next logical step for them to tell us when to die. We have grown so used to meekly accepting their edicts, even on what words we can and cannot use—"swamp" has virtually disappeared from the English language, replaced by "wetlands," as "bums" has been replaced by "the homeless," "sex" by "gender"—that it seems only fitting that they should now tell us when to die.

The new phrase is "the duty to die." The anointed have proclaimed this duty, so who are we ordinary people to question it? Former Colorado governor Richard Lamm has said that the elderly should "consider making room in the world for the young by simply doing with less medical care and letting themselves die."

Colorado didn't seem that desperately over-crowded to me, but Lamm is one of the voices of the anointed, so their arbitrary dogmas become well-known facts by sheer repetition.

In the *Hastings Center Report*, described as a journal of medical ethics, a medical ethicist says that "health care should be withheld even for those who want to live" if they have already lived beyond the politically correct number of years—which he suggests might be 75. He says that, after such a "full rich life" then "one is duty-bound to die."

There's more. Another medical ethicist would consider extending the limit to 80 years but, after that, medical care should be denied to all who have "lived out a natural life span."

You may wonder who these people are and who gave them the right to play God. But the answer is simple. They are legion and it is we who have supinely accepted their pronouncements on so many things for so long that they see no reason to limit how far they can go.

There was a time when Americans told people like this where they could go. But one of the many phrases to fade from our vocabulary is "None of your business!" Today, everything is everybody's business. The next step is for it to become the government's business.

This collectivist mentality has led to big noises being made in the media and in academia about whether corporate executives or professional athletes are being paid "too much." I don't know how many millions of dollars Derek Jeter gets paid for playing shortstop for the Yankees, but I do know that not one of those millions comes from me. That's between him and George Steinbrenner. It's none of my business.

How did we get sucked into collectivizing decisions that were once up to individuals? Purple prose is one factor. One of those who wants to see old-timers removed from the scene declares that the costs of keeping them alive are "a demographic, economic and medical avalanche." Melodramatic phrase-making has become the royal road to power.

What is far more of a threat than the little dictators who are puffed up with their own importance is the willingness of so many others to surrender their freedom and their money in exchange for phrases like "crisis" and "compassion." Will

America go down in history as the country which defeated collectivism in the 20th century and then became collectivist itself in the 21st century?

Collectivism takes on many guises and seldom uses its own real name. Words like "community" and "social" soothe us into thinking that collectivist decision-making is somehow higher and nobler than individual or "selfish" decision-making. But the cold fact is that communities do not make decisions. Individuals who claim to speak for the community impose their decisions on us all.

Collectivist dictation can occur from the local level to the international level, and the anointed push it at all levels. They want a bigger role for the UN, for the International Court of Justice at the Hague and for the European Union bureaucrats in Brussels. Anything except individual freedom.

You cannot even build or remodel your own home without finding yourself under the thumb of local bureaucrats and tangled in red tape. A couple who are trying to have a home built in coastal California are discovering that it takes far less time to build the house than it does to deal with the arbitrary edicts of local bureaucrats and the reams of local regulations. The husband has taken to singing in the shower: "We shall overcome some day. . ."

Maybe they will and maybe they won't. Maybe we are all destined to give up our freedom to those ruthless enough to take it from us—or glib enough to soothe us into handing it over to them.

SHOCKED
BY THE
OBVIOUS

The obvious makes headlines in California. Maybe this shows that a sense of reality or common sense is not something that can be taken for granted among Californians.

A recent headline stretching across the top of the front page announced that "Population dwarfs housing" in San Mateo County, on the San Francisco peninsula. The same headline would have applied throughout most of the state—and it should not have surprised anybody anywhere. But apparently a recent release of Census data brought much news that should not have been news.

Census statistics showed that the housing supply in San Mateo county grew only half as fast as the population. Should this have surprised anyone, given that more than two-thirds of the land in that country is off-limits for building anything? But, in California, there seems to be no connection in most people's minds between "open space" laws and housing so scarce that it is outrageously expensive. Often the very same people are passionately in favor of both "open space" and "affordable housing"—and see no conflict between these goals.

Nor do they see any conflict between arbitrary height restrictions on buildings and the clogged freeways that plague all of California. They would undoubtedly be shocked if told that open space and limits on building heights increase traffic deaths by forcing more people to drive greater distances from their dispersed housing to the places where they work. Such obvious common sense would undoubtedly produce headlines in California if someone would just go collect the statistics.

Whether the fear of looking like Manhattan would overcome the fear of death, if people stopped and thought about it, is not clear—because very few have stopped to think about the costs of most of California's sacred cows. Only recently have blackouts caused some to reconsider their automatic opposition to building power plants in general or nuclear power plants in particular.

For years, California's movie stars and environmental activists so demonized nuclear power plants that nobody bothered to find out what scientists thought or what the experience has been with nuclear power plants in Western Europe over the past decades. Facts play a very minor role in many decisions.

For example, to many Californians, the words "public power" still have a magic ring, despite the fact that people around the world have discovered the hard way that having politicians run economic activities produces disasters. That is why even left-wing governments in various countries have started selling government-owned enterprises to private industry. But few Californians either seek or welcome such facts. Nor are they likely to consider that Chernobyl was "public power."

Another headline on the same front page which announced that housing was lagging behind population growth also announced that the median age in the San Francisco Bay area was rising. Of course. As housing becomes ever more expensive, those who can afford it are increasingly restricted to those with higher incomes.

Contrary to political rhetoric, these are not some separate class of "the rich," but are simply people who have reached an age where their earnings have peaked, even though many of those very same people were counted among "the poor" in earlier years. Once you get past political rhetoric, it is easy to see why the most expensive places in the bay area tend to have the oldest ages and the poorest places the youngest ages.

In upscale Marin County, for example, the median age is 41. In San Mateo County, posh Portola Valley has a median age of 47.5, while run-down East Palo Alto, with a predominantly minority population, has a median age of just under 26.

Another headline, inside the same newspaper, declares: "Housing grows more nationwide than in state." Lots of things grow more nationwide than in California. That is because California politicians so heavily restrict, tax and micromanage so many economic activities that people are left freer to grow elsewhere.

The missing link in many Californians' thinking is the link between what they do and the consequences that follow. In California, you show what a good person you are by being in favor of all sorts of politically correct goals—and blithely disregarding the costs these goals will impose on others or the consequences for the whole society. That is why these obvious consequences produce such shocking headlines.

FAMILIES
AND
DICTATORS

In one sense, the Elian Gonzalez story is over. In another sense, it may be years before it is over, in the sense that the truth finally comes out.

Given how young Elian Gonzalez is and how old Fidel Castro is, it may be only a matter of time before Elian will be free to tell the truth, though that time may be measured in decades. How long the Castro regime will last after Castro himself is gone is problematical. But Cuba has no tradition of freedom to assure that it will become a democracy any time soon.

The one thing that is clear already is that this case was not about parental rights, which do not exist in Cuba, nor about "the rule of law," which did not exist in the Clinton administration. Judging by the polls, the American people do not understand that.

Part of the problem is that most Americans have no conception of a totalitarian dictatorship or the ruthlessness with which they use family members as hostages. This is nothing new, but our schools and colleges teach so little history that the public can hardly be expected to understand what an old and widespread pattern this is, among dictatorships of the left or right.

Back in the 1930s, for example, Nazi agents were infiltrating the many German organizations in Brazil. Those Germans in Brazil—many of them born in Brazil—who opposed Nazi takeovers of their organizations were reported to the Hitler government and their relatives back in Germany were subject to visits from the Gestapo.

Castro has retaliated against the brother of baseball pitcher Orlando Hernandez of the Yankees, who defected from Cuba. The family of a woman who defected from China a few years ago has likewise faced retaliation. Against this background, there is much overlooked significance in the fact that Castro has never let the entire Gonzalez family come to the United States at the same time. First the grandmothers came over while father Juan Miguel Gonzalez stayed behind. Then Juan Miguel came over with his wife and one son, while the grandmothers and another son stayed behind. But Castro always had his hostages in Cuba.

Those who do not understand this will have a hard time explaining some very strange things that went on during this long struggle over the fate of Elian Gonzalez.

Let's go back to the beginning, when this little boy was rescued from the sea, after the boat he was on sank, drowning his mother and others on board. Those who believe that his father was saying and doing what he freely wanted to say and do must face the fact that, with his son hospitalized after this traumatic experience, in a city that could be reached within the hour from Havana, the father waited for months before coming to the United States.

If that was the act of a free man, then he must be one of the most unfit parents around. More likely, he was as unfree as all the other people in Cuba.

What about what Juan Miguel Gonzalez said, that these were "distant" relatives in Miami, people he barely knew, who were holding his son against his father's wishes? It was Elian's uncle on his father's side. Are uncles distant relatives?

What is even more telling is that telephone records show that Juan Miguel Gonzalez phoned these "distant" relatives, whom he supposedly barely knew, just about the time when Elian and his mother were making a desperate attempt to reach American soil. The Miami family said that he asked them to take care of Elian but the father denies this. In Cuba, he had better deny it.

Then there were those grandmothers who came over, publicly asking for the return of Elian to Cuba. Yet, a Dominican nun who saw them privately in Miami said that these grandmothers showed fear like she had never seen before. The nun was at first in favor of returning Elian to Cuba and was, moreover, a friend of Janet Reno. But once she saw the fear of those grandmothers, she concluded that Castro was calling the shots and she wanted Elian kept out of his clutches.

The famous midnight raid was what sealed Elian's fate. Far from being made to uphold "the rule of law," that raid was made right after a court ruling that opened the door to a hearing requesting asylum for Elian. By seizing the boy at gunpoint and turning him over to his father, Janet Reno and the Clinton administration silenced Elian, who must now say whatever the Castro regime wants him to say. Those who want the truth will have to wait until Castro is gone.

THE
"AUTISM"
DRAGNET

The U.S. Department of Education and the National Institutes of Health have launched a campaign to get a government program created to "identify" children with autism at age two and then subject them to "intensive" early intervention for 25 hours a week or more. It sounds good, but so have so many other government programs that created more problems than they solved.

Just who is to "identify" these children and by what criteria? A legal case in Nebraska shows the dangers in creating a government-mandated dragnet that can subject all sorts of children to hours of disagreeable, ineffective or even counterproductive treatment for something they do not have.

A four-year old boy, whom we can call Bryan, was diagnosed as "autistic" and put into a program in which he grew worse instead of better, despite the protests of his parents. Eventually, these parents sued the school district, calling in as their expert witness Professor Stephen Camarata of Vanderbilt University.

Professor Camarata examined Bryan and concluded that he was not autistic and should not be kept in the program that was not doing him any good. However, the hearing officer sided with the school district, for reasons that are a chilling example of what can happen when bureaucratic criteria prevail.

According to the hearing officer: "The difficulty of the testimony of Dr. Camarata, is that it is obvious that he is frequently relying on a medical definition of autism, as opposed to the one contained in Nebraska Department of Education Rule 51." But, since autism is a medical condition, the problem is with the bureaucratic rule, not the medical definition.

When is a child autistic in Nebraska? According to the hearing officer, the "criteria established by the Nebraska Department of Education in order for a child to be verified as having autism" involve "varying degrees of atypical behavior" in a number of areas. These criteria reflect a lockstep view of how every child is supposed to develop.

Given that lockstep vision, "precocious or advanced skill development" in a child "while other skills may develop at normal or extremely depressed rates" is one of the criteria for autism. Similarly when the "order of skill acquisition frequently does not follow normal developmental patterns." In other words, if other kids can ride a tricycle before they can read and a particular kid can read before he can ride a tricycle, then he is in trouble.

Another sign of autism, according to bureaucratic rule 006.04B2b: "The child's behavior may vary from high levels of activity and responsiveness to low levels." If X turns him on and Y leaves him cold, then he is on his way to being labeled "autistic" in Nebraska.

Another sign of autism: "Speech and/or language are either absent, delayed, or disordered." This dragnet would bring in the great pianist Arthur Rubinstein, India's mathematical genius Ramanujan, Nobel Prize-winning economist Gary Becker, and physicists Richard Feynman, Edward Teller and Albert Einstein—among many others.

Meanwhile, back in Washington, people are pushing for a federal dragnet to find "autistic" children and subject them to "treatment" that none of us would want to undergo. They assure us that "experienced professionals" can identify autism in children as young as two years of age.

Even assuming that this is true, how many highly trained professionals are available to evaluate the vast numbers of children who would be caught in a nationwide "autism" dragnet? Would the whole country become Nebraska writ large?

Many children have already been labeled "autistic" or "retarded" on the basis of evaluations that lasted less then ten minutes—and many of these evaluations have later been contradicted, either by more highly qualified specialists or by the course of events as the child developed.

Parents need to seek out the best available medical and other evaluations of a child with problems. But that is very different from a federal dragnet controlled by armies of bureaucrats who can plague parents and children alike.

Parents of late-talking children have reported that they have been urged to allow their kids to be labeled "autistic" in order to get federal money that can be used for speech therapy. Maybe that has contributed to the "increase" in autism we hear about—which in turn has contributed to the stampede for a new federal program.

RACIAL
PROFILING
OF AUTHORS

Now that police departments are supposed to stop racial profiling, maybe it is time for book publishers and bookstores to
stop as well.

I first became aware of the racial profiling of authors when
I saw my book *Migrations and Cultures* in the black studies section of my local bookstore. Since the book is about migrations
from Europe and Asia, obviously the only reason for putting it
there was that the author is black.

Racial bean counters are asking publishers to tell them
which of their authors are black and no doubt some of these
publishers are complying. But the practical consequence of
this racial profiling is that a black author who writes a book
about cameras or cooking is liable to have his book put on a
bookstore shelf based on the race of the writer, rather than the
subject of the book. This means that readers who are looking
for books on cameras or cooking are unlikely to find his book
in the section where such books are kept.

Some people may actually think that they are doing black
writers a favor by setting up a black authors' section of a bookstore. But, with friends like these, who needs enemies? Black
writers, like white writers, want their books to reach the readers—and anything that interferes with that is bad news.

University of California Regent Ward Connerly found the

same practice in an east coast bookstore that I found on the west coast. His partly autobiographical and partly political book, *Creating Equal* was nowhere to be seen in either the biographical section of the bookstore or in the political section. It was on the shelves for "African-American Interest." The store manager said that this was done as a "service to the community."

What a service—putting a book where it is least likely to be found! If it is a service to any black writers, it is a service only to those who write exclusively for and about fellow blacks. But does either the black community or American society in general need a literary version of racial apartheid?

It is no service to readers either. Imagine that you are looking for a book on the history of military conquests and cannot find anything you like in the history section of your local bookstore—and that a book on that very subject by a black writer (yours truly, for example) is off in another part of the store.

Someone who stood in the black studies section of a major bookstore for 20 minutes reported that not a single white person entered that section during that time. Why would anyone want to put books where only a fraction of the public is likely to look—especially if it is a book on a subject of no special interest to that particular fraction?

It is bad enough that bookstores engage in the racial profiling of authors. But so do some publishers.

The ridiculous lengths to which publishers can carry racial profiling was demonstrated to me when copies of my recently published book *Basic Economics* were sent out to *Jet* magazine, the *Amsterdam News* and other black publications. After I complained, copies were then sent to the *Wall Street Journal* and other publications dealing with economics.

I had naively believed that publishers were not only in the

business of publishing books but also of selling them. But apparently keeping up with fads is considered more important.

The mindless political correctness of the racial bean counters has invaded and corrupted one institution after another. A recent advertisement in the *Chronicle of Higher Education* lists a job as "Vice-Provost for Diversity and Equal Opportunity." In other words, this job is being campus quota czar. You have reached the holy grail of "diversity" when you have black leftists, white leftists, female leftists and Hispanic leftists as professors.

Major corporations across the country have their affirmative action officials and many also have "diversity consultants" who come in and harangue the employees with the politically correct party line on race. Not since the days when the Nazis spoke of "Jewish science" has the idea been so widespread that race is destiny as far as ideas are concerned.

Only such an underlying assumption could create even the semblance of rationality to the notion that you are promoting "diversity" of viewpoints by having people of different skin colors on campus or in business—or with their books in different parts of bookstores.

CHANDRA
LEVY
CLUES

One of the clues in the Chandra Levy case that may have been dismissed too quickly was a call to the police on the morning of her disappearance, reporting a woman's scream heard in the building where she lived. This seems to have been disregarded as an unrelated event because it occurred hours before the time when Chandra Levy was supposed to have used her computer in her apartment.

But nobody actually saw her using the computer. All that is known is that the computer was used. If Chandra Levy was abducted hours earlier, whoever had her also had access to her keys. Why would such a person, or an accomplice, come back to that apartment and use a computer? Only to throw off the police.

Obviously, no ordinary street criminal would do that. Only someone with a vested interest in misleading the police would do it. But then, nothing else about the Chandra Levy case suggests that her disappearance was the work of a random street criminal.

Ordinary rapists, muggers and robbers do not go to such trouble to dispose of a body that a massive police dragnet fails to find it. Street criminals get what they want and then leave the scene before they are either caught by cops or recognized by witnesses.

Everything about the way Chandra Levy left her apartment suggests that she was going to meet someone she knew. Ordinarily she was very security conscious and took precautions, such as having her cell phone with her. Yet on this occasion she left everything behind in her apartment and took only her keys with her.

This does not necessarily mean that she knew the person who abducted her or killed her. She could have been lured to where that person was waiting by a message from someone she did know and trust, and who said that he or she would be at that place. Chandra might well have screamed when she was ambushed by somebody else.

All this suggests premeditation. Sometimes people have an argument that escalates out of control and leads to violence or death. But at such an emotional moment, one is not very likely to come up with a scheme for disposing of the body so cleverly that an army of cops cannot find it.

Murders are all too common. But murders in which the body cannot be found are much rarer. There has to be some compelling reason why a killer does not just flee the scene of the crime.

Obviously, if the crime occurred in the killer's home or on his job, then the body must be moved. But, if it happened somewhere else, then the dangers of hanging around or carting a body around would have to be weighed against whatever advantage could be gotten by hiding the body.

What do you gain by hiding the body? In some cases, it may be possible to hide the fact that any crime was committed. If a globe-trotting reporter were murdered in London and the body never found, then that reporter might just be regarded as missing in action anywhere around the world. But that was impossible in the case of Chandra Levy.

As an intern whose term was up at a particular time, and

whose parents were expecting her back in California shortly afterwards, Chandra Levy's disappearance was bound to be noticed, whether a body turned up or not. With the passage of time, the likelihood of an accident would have to decline to the vanishing point and foul play left as the only reasonable conclusion.

If her death was caused by someone who knew her, then that person would also know this. Thus there would be no point in trying to conceal the very existence of a crime. All that could be concealed would be the identity of whoever was responsible. Misleading the police about the time at which her abduction happened might be worth spending some time at her computer or having someone else spend time there.

In any event, someone obviously thought it was very important that her body not be found. But why? If her body were found in a park or on the street with a fatal gunshot wound, for example, how much of a clue would that be? Enough to take the risks of spending time finding a secure place to dispose of her remains?

What would make her body a bigger clue would be if she were pregnant. That could point the police toward whoever was responsible for her death. Moreover, pregnancy could have set in motion a chain of events that led someone to feel a need to get rid of her permanently. Pregnant young women can cause big trouble, especially if they feel betrayed by whoever was responsible.

BARRY

AND

THE BABE

This season, Barry Bonds has been a Giant in more than name. While baseball fans and the media have been focussed on his record-breaking home-run feats, far less attention has been paid to his other feats that have been even more spectacular—and, in fact, unique.

Barry Bonds is the first batter in the entire history of the National League—going back into the 19th century—to have a slugging average over .800. The only other player in the history of baseball to slug over .800 was Babe Ruth, who did it two seasons in a row.

In other words, a slugging average of .800 is rarer than a batting average of .400. The last player to hit .400—Ted Williams—did it 60 years ago. But Ruth slugged .800 twenty years before that—and nobody else has done it again until this year.

Slugging averages tell you more than either batting averages or home run totals. As far as batting averages are concerned, a bunt single and a tape-measure home run are the same. But they are rarely the same in their effect on the outcome of a ball game.

The total number of home runs is not the whole story either. The year that Roger Maris broke Babe Ruth's record for home runs in a season, Mickey Mantle actually hit home runs in a higher percentage of his times at bat. It is just that Mantle was walked more than Maris. A big reason why Maris was walked less than a hundred times that year was that Mantle was on deck. Walking Maris would just get you in deeper and deeper.

Just as batting averages count hits in proportion to your times at bat, slugging averages count your total bases in proportion to your times at bat. If you hit a single and a double in five times at bat, that's three total bases and a slugging average of .600. That slugging average for a whole season is rarer than a batting average of .300.

A slugging average of .700 is of course even rarer. Some of the great sluggers of all time—Joe DiMaggio, Hank Aaron, Willie Mays—never reached a slugging average of .700 in even their best seasons. So a slugging average over .800 is practically unheard of.

What does an .800 slugging average mean? It means 8 total bases every ten times at bat— all season long. You can get 8 total bases with two singles, a double and a home run. Or you can do it with two home runs or four doubles or other combinations. But, however you do it, it is hard to keep on doing it for a whole season. Only Barry and the Babe have done that.

It is not coincidental that Ruth and Bonds each holds his respective league's season records for being walked. These are not the kind of guys you can afford to pitch to when the game is on the line. It is significant that Bonds hit his 70th home run in the last inning of a game where the score was 9 to 2. He had been walked again and again earlier in that game and in previous games when the score was close.

Where does this incredible season put Bonds among the all-time greats? It certainly moves him up the list but one season is not a whole career. Like Roger Maris, Bonds hit over 20 home runs more in his record-breaking season than he did in any other season. Will he turn out to be a one-year wonder, like Maris?

This is not to say that Bonds would not have been a star player, even if he had never had this spectacular season. He would have been headed for Cooperstown anyway. Maris too was an outstanding player and had won the Most Valuable Player award the year before breaking the home run record, as well as in that year.

But if you are talking about being up there in the rarefied atmosphere of Babe Ruth, that is another story. Bonds never had a slugging average of .700 before this year. Mark McGwire reached that level twice and Babe Ruth nine times. Ruth's lifetime slugging average was .690, a level Bonds never reached in his best season before this year.

Take nothing away from Barry Bonds. He hit home runs this year with a greater frequency, in proportion to his times at bat, than anyone in the history of baseball. He homered once every 6.5 official times at bat, compared to once every 7.3 at bats for McGwire and once every 9 at bats for Ruth in his best seasons.

While Bonds' incredible performance gave new prominence to slugging averages, Ruth's lifetime dominance in that statistic makes clear that the Babe was still the greatest all-around slugger of them all, regardless of how many home runs others have hit.

MEDIA
FRAUD

Media bias is no longer news. Poll after poll has shown that the vast majority of journalists vote for Democrats, even though the country as a whole is pretty evenly split between the two major parties.

By itself, there is nothing wrong with this. It becomes a problem when media bias becomes media fraud. Media bias in editorials and columns is one thing. Media fraud in reporting "facts" in news stories is something else.

Three excellent and devastating new books on media fraud have been published this year, naming names and turning over rocks to show what is crawling underneath. These books are *Coloring the News* by William McGowan, *Bias* by Bernard Goldberg, and *It Ain't Necessarily So* by David Murray, Joel Schwartz and S. Robert Lichter.

In even the best known and most prestigious media outlets—the *New York Times* and "60 Minutes," for example—crucial facts have been left out of news stories when those facts would have undermined or destroyed a liberal argument. Conversely, false claims have been widely reported as facts in the media when those claims supported the liberal vision of the world.

A classic media fraud was the 1996 story of a wave of arsons directed against black churches by racists. It made headlines across the country and was featured on network television news. It sparked indignant editorials and angry outbursts from black activists. The President of the United States recalled his own sadness as a child at the burning down of black churches in Arkansas.

In the end, however, the whole thing turned out to be completely false. Those few journalists who bothered to check out the facts found that there were no facts to support this story and that what facts there were completely refuted it. Even a commission appointed by President Clinton reached the same conclusion. Moreover, not a single black church in Arkansas had burned down during Bill Clinton's childhood.

When this front page fraud was finally exposed, the new story was buried as a small item back on page 20 of the *New York Times*.

William McGowan's *Coloring the News* offers the best explanation for such journalistic malpractice. Many news organizations have created special editorial office caucuses consisting exclusively of black, Hispanic, feminist, or homosexual journalists, who decide how the news about their respective constituencies will be reported—or whether it will be reported at all.

For example, when a homosexual man was attacked and killed by anti-gay hoodlums, that was huge, front-page news across the country. But when two homosexuals lured a boy next door into their home and then raped and killed him, at about the same time, that was widely ignored, as if it had never happened. Similarly biased treatment has appeared when it came to reporting on corrupt black politicians like D.C. mayor Marion Barry or the dangerous double standards used for women in the military—standards which have already led to death in training and may cost still more lives in actual combat.

The issue is not what various journalists or news organizations's editorial views are. The issue is the transformation of news reporting into ideological spin, along with self-serving taboos and outright fraud.

While William McGowan's book seems the most perceptive of these three, all are very valuable and each has its own special emphasis. *It Ain't Necessarily So* focuses on media irresponsibility when reporting on medical and scientific issues, while *Bias* focuses more on the actions and the cast of characters at CBS News, where its author worked for many years. But all three of these books provide a real education on media fraud, which is infinitely more important than media bias.

Democratic nations are especially vulnerable to misinformation. The media in a totalitarian country may tell as many lies as it wants to, but that does not affect the decisions made for the country by its dictator or its ruling party, which has access to the truth, even if the masses do not. But, in a country where the masses choose their leaders and influence policies, a fraudulent press can mislead the voters into national disaster.

THE INSULATION
OF
THE LEFT

Nature lovers marvel at the fact that newly hatched turtles instinctively head for the sea. But that is no more remarkable than the fact that people on the political left instinctively head for occupations in which their ideas do not have to meet the test of facts or results.

While many studies have documented the predominance of the political left in the academic world, the exceptional areas where they do not have such predominance are precisely those areas where you cannot escape from facts and results— the sciences, engineering, mathematics and athletics.

By contrast, no area of academia is more dominated by the left than the humanities, where there are no facts to challenge the fantasies that abound. Leftists head for similar fact-free zones outside of academia.

Philanthropy, for example, is another field in which facts take a back seat to beliefs and emotions. When you are handing out money, you call the tune. It doesn't matter if other people have the facts on their side if you have the big bucks on yours.

When the foundations put their money behind bilingual education or global warming, then all sorts of conferences, organizations and movements will emerge to carry forth their message. Leftists flock to foundations, including those set up with money donated by conservative businessmen.

When these foundations give big bucks to finance bilingual education programs and propaganda, or bankroll "global warming" hysteria, they cannot be forced to confront facts about the counterproductive effects of bilingual education or asked to prove that the globe has warmed by a single degree in 20 years.

Fiction and opinion are likewise dominated by the political left. If you can tell a good yarn, whether in a book or a motion picture, the only test you face is whether people will buy the book or go see the movie.

On TV talk shows, what matters is whether you can talk the talk that keeps people tuned in. You may scare the daylights out of them about fictitious dangers in apples or beef without a speck of evidence that you know what you are talking about. But, so long as it sounds good, that's all that matters.

Any engineer, businessmen or athletic coach who knew no more about what he was doing than the talking heads on TV or foundation officials have to know would be heading for disaster in no time. When your bridge collapses or your business goes bankrupt or your team gets beaten again and again, you are history.

Nowhere are half-baked ideas more safe from facts than in government. When the Equal Employment Opportunity Commission assumes that statistical "imbalances" in a company's workforce show discrimination, the only test of that assumption is whether federal judges share it.

If the EEOC and the courts share this same assumption, then employers are out of luck—perhaps to the tune of millions of dollars—if their workforce does not fit the prevailing preconceptions. Even if in fact the accused employer couldn't care less about the complexion, the nationality or the bedroom habits of his employees, that doesn't matter. What matters is what those with power choose to believe.

It doesn't matter whether factual studies show that "whole language" and "whole math" methods of teaching lead to lower test scores in these subjects. What matters is whether those with the money and the power in the Department of Education happen to like these notions—or are willing to cater to the teachers' unions that like them.

One of the reasons why government absorbs so much money and takes on ever-increasing powers is that it is home to so many people whose beliefs could not withstand the draconian tests of science, the marketplace or a scoreboard. What we the taxpayers are ultimately paying for is their insulation from reality, as they pursue the heady pleasures of power.

As if that were not enough, the left promotes the idea that there is something wiser and nobler about having decisions made by third parties who pay no price for being wrong. That is called "public service" and it will undoubtedly be hyped in college commencement speeches this year—as it is every year—despite scandalous revelations in Washington or decades of economic failure and monumental human tragedies in left-wing governments around the world.

W. GLENN CAMPBELL
(1924–2001)

He could be generous, he could be irascible, but he could never be anything other than Glenn Campbell. During his long career, and from his retirement in 1989 until his recent death on November 24th, no one else was ever described as being "like Glenn Campbell." He was an original.

It would be an understatement to call Glenn Campbell controversial and a virtual impossibility to keep track of all his battles, including those with more than one administration of Stanford University, on whose campus his Hoover Institution was and is located.

There was a Hoover Institution before Glenn Campbell became its director in 1960, but it was he who added world-class scholars to its huge library and massive archives, making it a think tank that would eventually be ranked number one among the think tanks of the world by the distinguished British magazine *The Economist*.

He also brought in the millions of dollars that supported their research and caused the institution to grow in size and in stature. But his achievement went even beyond that.

In an era when academic thinking was almost exclusively on the political left, the Hoover Institution became a refuge for top scholars who were out of step with that orientation, and who were therefore persona non grata at colleges and universities for which they were academically qualified but politically blackballed.

While the media almost invariably referred to the Hoover Institution as "conservative" or "right-wing," a survey of its scholars during the 1980s found that there were slightly more Democrats than Republicans. In the surrounding Stanford University faculty—as with faculties at most universities—there were whole departments without a single Republican, at a time when the country was almost evenly split between the two parties.

Glenn Campbell liked to say that the Stanford faculty was leaning so far to the left that the upright scholars at the Hoover Institution seemed to be leaning far to the right.

While the Hoover scholars included such icons of free market economics as Milton Friedman, George Stigler, and Gary Becker—all Nobel Prize winners—they also included Nobel Prize-winning economist Kenneth Arrow, whose orientation was very different. These were all academically-based scholars who were affiliated with the Hoover Institution under one arrangement or another, spending varying amounts of time there. Other leading scholars were exclusively affiliated with the Hoover Institution and permanently in residence.

These included Peter Duignan and Lewis Gann, whose monumental histories of Africa were internationally recognized for their scholarship, but who were never on the faculties of any university. Given the benefits of being at the Hoover Institution—someone described it as having a MacArthur Foundation fellowship all the time—it was probably no great loss to them. But it was a huge loss to innumerable college and university students who would never hear anything that challenged the "politically correct" version of African history.

Other scholars in residence included the distinguished British historian Robert Conquest, whose monumental book,

Harvest of Sorrow, spelled out the horrors of the man-made famine in the Ukraine which took millions of lives in the 1930s. While this famine was denied, not only by the Soviet government and its fellow travelers in the West, and down-played or widely ignored by much of the intelligentsia, when the official Soviet files were finally opened under Gorbachev, it turned out that even more people had died than Conquest had estimated.

In short, the Hoover Institution was not only a refuge for scholars who refused to march in ideological lockstep with the fashions of the times, it was a refuge for ideas that were largely banished from academia and the media, but which could not be obliterated so long as they had a base from which incon-venient facts and analyses could be developed and published in books, articles, monographs and op-ed columns.

It was Glenn Campbell's contribution to America to pre-serve a genuine diversity that so many academics talked about but refused to permit on their campuses. That will be his en-during monument.

PART VII

RANDOM THOUGHTS

RANDOM
THOUGHTS

Ad for a ski resort: "If swimming is so healthful, why are whales so fat?"

Scientists are now putting jellyfish genes in monkeys. I don't know what they are trying to produce, but they could end up producing academic administrators.

The first big Washington scandal of the 20th century was the Teapot Dome scandal of 1921, which led three members of the Harding administration to commit suicide. Today, they would just consult their lawyers and spinmeisters, and then start making the rounds of the talk shows in order to confuse the issues.

We call too many people "sick" who are in fact sickening. And we call too many young criminals "troubled youths," when in fact they are trouble to other people, while enjoying themselves.

If Yogi Berra actually said all the things that have been attributed to him, when did he ever have any time left to play baseball?

In a democracy, why should one group of citizens carry more

weight than a similar number of other citizens, just because they are willing to take to the streets and block traffic?

Someone said that human beings are the only creatures that blush—and the only ones that need to.

It is bad enough that so many of our public schools offer nothing to challenge smart students. What adds insult to injury is that, when these students become bored and restless, this boredom is given the fancy name "attention deficit hyperactivity disorder" and the students are drugged with Ritalin.

There are too many mush heads around these days for the law to continue to require unanimous jury verdicts.

Because of the neglect of history in our educational system, most people have no idea how many of the great American fortunes were created by people who were born and raised in worse poverty than the average welfare-recipient today.

The problem with trying to restore every group to its own historic "homeland" is that so many parts of the earth have been homelands to different groups at different periods of history. New Orleans, for example, has belonged to four different nations that we know about, not counting how often it may have changed hands before Europeans arrived in the hemisphere and began keeping written records.

The media continue to take seriously, and provide free publicity for, people who call themselves "consumer advocates" or "environmentalists," even though there are no qualifications required for these roles. All it takes are a big mouth, a big ego, a disdain for inconvenient facts and an ignorance of economics.

It is amazing how many of the horrors of the 20th century were a result of charismatic quacks misleading millions of people to their own doom. What is even more amazing is that, after a century that saw the likes of Hitler, Lenin and Mao, we still see no need to distrust charisma as a basis for choosing leaders, either in politics or in numerous organizations and movements.

When Japan sells us enough cars to buy Rockefeller Center, that is just another even exchange. But accounting rules call it an international trade "deficit" because the cars crossed international borders, while Rockefeller Center stayed put. Yet the media, politicians and the intelligentsia spread alarms because they pay more attention to the word than to the reality.

It used to be said that it is better to light one candle than to curse the darkness. Today, we admire those who curse the candle—because it is not perfect, not free, not whatever the complainers want it to be.

When it comes to the future of this country, what is scarier than any bad policies or bad leaders is the sheep-like willingness of so many Americans to repeat slogans, follow demagogues and even allow their own children to be dosed with Ritalin or sent to serve food to bums in the name of "community service," without questioning the right of other people to do these things.

Beware of people who discuss foreign policy in terms of "relieving international tensions." You can always relieve tensions by surrendering. We have done it on issue after issue.

The average black family has been in America longer than the average white family. Why then should blacks be hyphenated as African-Americans when they are more centuries removed from Africa than most Europeans are from Europe? Does anyone speak of European-Americans? How long should a hyphen persist?

Taxpayers have a right to complain about the runaway cost of the welfare state, but its worst damage has been done by promoting counterproductive lifestyles and creating a whole class of hustlers who know how to game the system, as well as an army of loudmouths who know how to intimidate politicians into giving them more of the same.

Why is it that people who are against the cigarette companies for selling a product with the potential to kill raise no similar objections to those who make equipment for sky-diving, white-water rafting, mountain climbing and other activities that also involve people risking their lives for the sake of the enjoyment they get?

Why is it that some people who are opposed to the government's giving money to faith-based organizations are also in favor of the government's providing money for "mental health," when much of what shrinks do is based on faith, rather than on empirical evidence?

There has been so much gushing about the supposed benefits of "diversity" that we have become conditioned to respond automatically to the word, much as Pavlov's dog was conditioned to respond to the ringing of a bell. But evidence is neither asked nor given.

Those who disdain wealth as a worthy goal for an individual or a society seem not to realize that wealth is the only thing that can prevent poverty.

Have you ever known a time when there was so much talk about ethics—or so little practice of it?

The great ideological divide is between those who believe that theories should be adjusted to reality and those who believe that reality must be adjusted to fit their theories. Many of the horrors of the 20th century were created by the latter. And such people are still with us, in many movements.

Some people go to desperate lengths to avoid making an estimate. They say that it all depends, that there are many factors, that there are no guarantees, that unforeseen things could happen. Don't we already know all that? Isn't that why we call it an estimate, rather than a guaranteed certainty?

Why does everything that the government does become so complicated? Because there are more than 500 members of Congress, each one of them with his or her own pet notions. Many of these notions have to be incorporated into legislation to get a majority in favor of any bill. The result is a complicated monstrosity.

Everyone is supposed to be "non-judgmental" these days. But how can it be wrong to judge, when such a statement is itself a judgment?

We have all heard about the "mid-life crisis" but did you know that there is now a book out titled *QuarterLife Crisis*? It is about how tough it is to turn 25. Apparently everybody has to whine about something.

Any politician who can be elected only by turning Americans against other Americans is too dangerous to be elected.

Too many people fail to see the fatal difference between having a government create rules that apply to all—"a government of laws and not of men"—and having government officials choose the destinies of individuals and groups, whether through affirmative action, "targeted tax cuts," or special subsidies or special taxes for those who happen to be in or out of favor in Washington.

No individual and no generation has had enough personal experience to ignore the vast experience of the human race that is called history. Yet most of our schools and colleges today pay little attention to history. And many of our current policies repeat mistakes that were made, time and again, in the past with disastrous results.

Some people seem to think that the answer to all of life's imperfections is to create a government agency to correct them. If that is your approach, then go straight to totalitarianism. Do not pass "Go." Do not collect $200.

Just what part of "Congress shall make no law" don't politicians understand? The First Amendment forbids Congress from passing any law that will even "abridge" the freedom of speech. Yet campaign finance reform laws would flat-out forbid certain speech by certain organizations on the eve of elections.

If you want to see the poor remain poor, generation after generation, just keep the standards low in their schools and make excuses for their academic shortcomings and personal misbehavior. But please don't congratulate yourself on your compassion.

The very same people who say that the government has no right to interfere with sexual activity between consenting adults believe that the government has every right to interfere with economic activity between consenting adults.

The welfare state is the greatest confidence racket of all time. The government takes your money in taxes and then turns around and spends some of it to give you things. For this, you feel dependent on them, when in fact they are dependent on you.

Those who consider themselves deep thinkers like to point out that other societies have different values than those found in American society, as if that proves that values are arbitrary and unnecessary. But some other societies eat very different foods than those that Americans eat. Yet does anyone imagine that this proves food to be something arbitrary and unnecessary?

People who pride themselves on having ideas often fail to understand that only after ideas have been filtered through real-world experience do we know whether they are right or wrong. Most turn out to be wrong.

When my wife dragged me to a department store to buy myself some new clothes, the salesman there said: "Some men would wear their clothes until they were rags if they didn't have wives."

No matter what you say, some people will hear only what they want to hear.

Old age at least gives me an excuse for not being very good at things that I was not very good at when I was young.

It is amazing how many people consider it an answer to criticism to call it "bashing."

Apologizing for sins committed by other people in the past seems to have become a political vogue. Considering all the wrongs committed around the world for centuries—against people of every race, color, creed, national origin, and sexual orientation—if we are going to apologize for all that, we are not going to have any time left to get anything else done.

The promotion of "self-esteem" in our schools has been so successful that people feel free to spout off about all sorts of things—and see no reason why their opinions should not be taken as seriously as the views of people who actually know what they are talking about.

Being in the right place at the right time plays a bigger role in our lives than many are ready to admit. Earle Combs played center field for the New York Yankees for more than a decade and had the same lifetime batting average as Joe DiMaggio (.325). Yet Combs is virtually forgotten, because he played in the shadow of Babe Ruth and Lou Gehrig.

Ours may become the first civilization destroyed, not by the power of our enemies, but by the ignorance of our teachers and the dangerous nonsense they are teaching our children. In an age of artificial intelligence, they are creating artificial stupidity.

One of the great meaningless phrases of our times is: "I take full responsibility." This does not mean that you are prepared to pay the consequences for what you have done. On the contrary, this statement is usually offered instead of taking the consequences.

The political left loves to refer disdainfully to people who have "faith in the free market." Mountains of empirical evidence

from countries around the world on the superior performances of free markets are thus dismissed as mere faith. Meanwhile, the repeated failures of government-run economies are
attributed to personal mistakes by Stalin, Mao or others—
thereby preserving the left's faith in political control of economic decisions, if only the right people were in charge.

Real teaching is real work. That is why schools go in for so
many "activities" and "projects" instead.

The heaviest Miss America was supposed to have weighed 143
pounds. That was back in the days when women were women.

A recent poll shows that a majority of blacks, whites, Asians
and Hispanics do not think the Census should be classifying
people as black, white, Asian and Hispanic.

Advocates of rent control and tenants' rights laws often complain about dishonest and unscrupulous landlords. It never
seems to occur to them that, when laws make it impossible for
honest and decent landlords to make a living, it is virtually
inevitable that many rent-controlled buildings will end up in
the hands of people who are neither honest nor decent, since
they are the only ones who can make any money out of them.

The dogma that no culture is superior to any other is contradicted by facts at every turn. Virtually every culture is superior
to some other cultures at something. How many cultures can
brew beer like the Germans, create wine like the French or
make Sake like the Japanese?

Virtually every education guru of the 20th century, from John
Dewey in the past to Howard Gardner today, has written in a
vague, lofty and slippery style. Whether this has been due to
confusion, camouflage or cowardice, what has been avoided

at all costs have been straightforward statements that could be checked against the facts.

Big-spending, big-government liberals know that they will have a hard time being elected as what they are, so they pretend to be something else. Then, when their opponents expose their phoniness, that is greeted with horror in the media as "negative campaigning." Have we become so squeamish that we would rather elect someone to high office on false pretenses than hear an unpleasant truth?

Bumper sticker: "Gun Control: Use both hands."

In the American legal system, the accused is presumed to be innocent until proven guilty. To some on the political left, he is presumed to be innocent even after being proven guilty.

Among the many dishonest polls whose results are reported solemnly in the media is one that said there were "4,000 dead children" as a result of gun violence and then asked: "Should gun laws be seriously tightened?" Most of the "children" referred to in such statistics are teenage gang members, not toddlers who find a loaded gun in the closet. These teenage criminals are not about to be deterred by gun laws.

Our national problems usually do not cause nearly as much harm as the solutions.

How can "hate crimes" laws be constitutional, when the 14th Amendment specifies "equal protection of the laws" for all, not special protection for special groups?

Government officials have a lot of nerve to be sounding off about the "greed" of oil companies. The federal government alone gets several times as much in taxes from every gallon of gasoline as oil companies get in profit. But government is never considered greedy, not even when it takes over half the money of some people who have died, instead of letting it go to their children.

While American students go to school almost as many days as students in other countries, the number of hours they spend on core subjects like history, math and science in high school is less than half the hours spent on these subjects in Japan, Germany or France.

There is nothing egalitarian about lower intellectual standards in our schools. Children from more fortunate homes will get higher standards in those homes. It is the other children who most need some outside source of the things necessary to re-alize their potential.

World War II films on the History Channel show the desperate courage of the men who fought then. What a painful contrast with the cheap cowardice of the politicians who got them into such a mess in the first place.

We used to have day care centers back in my time. We called them homes.

When the history of grossness is written, our times may well be called its golden age.

If a politician had a coat of arms, it would probably be a weasel on a background of waffles and mush.

Sometimes the hardest thing about paying the monthly bills is finding them in the first place, under all the junk mail.

Nobody would put as little thought and effort into buying an automobile as they put into deciding who to elect as President of the United States.

A friend from India told me that a countryman of his said: "I want to go to America. I want to see a country where poor people are fat."

Our foreign aid may not have helped many Third World countries, but it has probably helped the economy of Switzerland, where many Third World despots keep their own bank accounts.

It has long been said that the President of the United States—whoever he is—is president of all the people. But he is not president of all the fish, reptiles and other supposedly endangered species that are constantly taking precedence over human needs.

It is amazing how many of the intelligentsia call it "greed" to want to keep what you have earned, but not greed to want to take away what somebody else has earned, and let politicians use it to buy votes.

We have tears for when we have nothing else.

An American flag is more likely to fly on a mobile home than on a mansion.

Someone said that the light at the end of the tunnel could be a freight train heading your way.

As someone who has worked both in private industry and in academia, whenever I hear about academics wanting to teach ethics to people in business, I want to puke.

Big differences that can be worked out are less dangerous than small differences that can't be.

Too many people in the media seem to think that being objective means criticizing "both sides," when in fact it means an unbiased search for the truth. You can do objective research on the Nazis and then conclude that they were pretty rotten people.

The strongest argument for socialism is that it sounds good. The strongest argument against socialism is that it doesn't work. But those who live by words will always have a soft spot in their hearts for socialism because it sounds so good.

Whatever you may think about the death penalty, it has the lowest recidivism rate of any of the ways of fighting crime.

Some things are so obvious that, if you have to explain them, you can't explain them.

Guess who said this: "Yes, the president should resign. He has lied to the American people, time and time again, and betrayed their trust." It was said by Bill Clinton—about Richard Nixon.

Few skills are so well rewarded as the ability to convince parasites that they are victims.

The grand fallacy of the political left is that decisions are better made by third parties who pay no price for being wrong. Much of the 20th century has been taken up proving how tragically mistaken that theory is, all around the world. But those who want to be the third-party decision-makers still remain undaunted.

Proposals for reform are often dismissed because they have no "realistic" chance of being adopted. But none of the major reforms of the past had any realistic chance of being adopted when they were first proposed.

Sign in a store window: "Free ride in a police car for shoplifters."

Bumper sticker on a van in Berkeley: "Thank you for not breeding."

The kinds of people we need in government are precisely the kinds of people who are most reluctant to go into government—people who understand the inherent dangers of power and feel a distaste for using it, but who may do so for a few years as a civic duty. The worst kind of people to have in government are those who see it as a golden opportunity to impose their own superior wisdom and virtue on others.

Jack Dempsey once said that nobody who had any other way of making a living would become a professional boxer and Joe DiMaggio said that no boy from a rich family ever made the big leagues.

While waiting for my wife to get ready so that we could go out, I told her that I was pacing back and forth. "That's good exercise," she said.

When will people in the media realize that government is not about the careers of politicians or the maneuvers of special interest groups—which is all that many of them seem to want to talk about? Is it so hard for media people to inform themselves on the substance of the issues themselves and the impact of policies on a quarter of a billion Americans who live outside the Beltway?

One of the scariest things about our times is how easy it is to scare people and start a political stampede. There are people who could be upset if they were told that half of all Americans earn less than the median income—though of course that is the way median income is defined.

Ethnic identity movements are ways of getting rid of minor discomforts by creating major catastrophes.

One of the reasons for conspiracy theories is an assumption that people in high places always know what they are doing. When they do something that makes no sense, devious reasons are imagined by conspiracy theorists, when in fact it may be due to plain old ignorance and incompetence.

So many parents today are so permissive that they can hardly be called parents. Perhaps "adult hosts" might be a more accurate term.

Do you know of any other written agreement that can be ended by one side as easily as a marriage?

The right to die all too readily becomes the right to kill—especially since those who are dead cannot dispute the story told by those who are still living.

Social Security forces individuals to save for their old age. But it also enables the government to spend those savings immediately, so that the country as a whole is not saving anything this way. That is why old-age pensions will have to be paid from money taken from others in the future.

There was a time when we honored those who created the prosperity and the freedom that we enjoy. Today we honor the complainers and sue the creators. Perhaps that is inevitable in an era when we no longer count our blessings, but instead count all our unfulfilled wishes.

Will Rogers said that the way to end highway congestion is to have the government build the cars and private industry build the highways.

If we could take our great grandparents around on a tour of America as it is today, they would not only be astonished by all the things we have, they would be even more astonished by all the whining because we don't have more.

By being too squeamish to punish "first offenders," we are being cruel in the long-run. Instead of nipping some criminal careers in the bud, we let young people think the law is a joke—which can then lead them into more crimes and eventually hard time in prison.

According to *Sports Illustrated*, nearly half the high school sports injuries that lead to paralysis or death occur among cheerleaders.

You seldom see the word "risque" any more. We have gotten so gross that the word would have no meaning now.

All too often, we do smart things only after exhausting every conceivable dumb thing we could have done.

My favorite diet drink has zero calories. But it makes me so hungry that I eat like a horse.

Has anyone ever asked what a full professor is full of? In some trendy new fields, the title "empty professor" would be more appropriate.

Do you sometimes feel that you are necessary but not sufficient?

Few things are more disgusting than seeing squeamish people giving themselves airs of moral superiority because they lack the guts to do what needs to be done to preserve the institutions and the society from which they benefit.

If we can't get rid of so-called "vocational education" in our public schools, then at least we can have the honesty to stop calling it vocational education and call it what it is—non-academic courses. These courses are often of no use in any vocation.

The welfare state is the oldest con game in the world. First you take the people's money quietly and then you give some of it back to them flamboyantly.

If politicians were serious about day care for children, instead of just sloganizing about it, nothing they could do would improve the quality of child care more than by lifting the heavy burden of taxation that forces so many families to have both parents working.

If there is one common denominator among public school teachers and administrators, it is that the very idea of testing their beliefs against evidence never seems to occur to them. The educational dogmas of the day simply reign supreme until new dogmas come along.

The least productive people are usually the ones who are most in favor of holding meetings.

Many vices are just virtues that have been carried too far.

The only thing better than "hands-on" experience is hands-off experience—enough experience to understand that some things will turn out better if left alone.

Teachers who think that they have a right to use other people's children as guinea pigs for social experiments should be fired.

When someone defined "baroque" as "not having enough Monet," I said that I thought Monet was the root of all evil. To this a reader replied: "There you Gogh again. It's the 'love' of Monet that's the root of all evil."

Franklin D. Roosevelt called December 7th, 1941 "a date that will live in infamy." Not at Harvard, Stanford or Princeton, where less than half of all students interviewed knew the date of the Japanese attack on Pearl Harbor.

The political left always wants to equalize expenditures per school or school districts. But they show no interest in equalizing expenditures per child, regardless of what school that child attends, including private schools that accept vouchers.

Karl Spence of the *Chattanooga Free Press* aptly characterizes the views of the liberal intelligentsia as: "Let my conscience be your guide."

One of the common failings among honorable people is a failure to appreciate how thoroughly dishonorable some other people can be and how dangerous it is to trust them.

The next time some academics tell you how important "diversity" is, ask how many Republicans there are in their sociology department.

Sign on a San Francisco automobile dealer's wall: "We cheat the other guy and pass the savings on to you."

They say cream rises to the top. However, among government employees, the cream tends to leave after a few years, allowing mediocrity to rise to the top.

"Entitlement" is not only the opposite of achievement, it undermines incentives to do all the hard work that leads to achievement.

One of the most fashionable notions of our times is that social problems like poverty and oppression breed wars. Most wars, however, are started by well-fed people with time on their hands to dream up half-baked ideologies or grandiose ambitions, and to nurse real or imagined grievances.

Any philanthropist who is in doubt as to the best place to put his money to help others should invest in the private economy, where it will serve purposes determined by the consuming public, rather than by coteries of self-righteous and self-important people spending other people's money.

A politician once declared: "Even if I said that, I was misquoted."

Some husbands are insanely jealous—and some are sanely jealous.

Someone has claimed that men think about sex every 8 seconds. The way some women dress suggests that they want to make it more frequent than that.

If you have always believed that everyone should play by the same rules and be judged by the same standards, that would have gotten you labeled a radical 60 years ago, a liberal 30 years ago and a racist today.

People who oppose school vouchers say that we should improve the public schools instead—but they never specify any time limit. Are we to continue through all eternity to pour more and more billions of dollars down a bottomless pit, without regard to whether or not any improvement results and without ever considering any alternatives?

Liberalism is totalitarianism with a human face.

Many of the people who are called "the homeless" could more accurately be called "the rentless." Often they have a roof over their head, but someone else is paying for it, usually the taxpayers. Similarly, many of those who are called "the hungry" are in fact being fed every day, but at someone else's expense.

One of the most ridiculous causes of automobile accidents is that some people are very eager to save very small amounts of time.

Letter from a working mother whose children are now grown: "Today we have our payoff. We live in a beautiful home and I drive a new Cadillac. I have literally everything I want. My husband buys me enormous gifts. People say we are rich. I would burn my house to the ground if I could go back to that day at the day care when I pulled away from clinging hands and cried all the way to work."

There are many things that are much easier to maintain than to repair—ranging from automobiles to people's confidence in you.

For those who like to learn from other people's mistakes, here is a recent experience of mine: Having decided that I wasn't getting enough exercise, I went out and got too much exercise. The net result was a week on crutches and no exercise at all.

If you don't believe in the innate unreasonableness of human beings, just try raising children.

War makes me respect soldiers and despise politicians.

The kind of people who talk about the "root causes" of crime never include leniency.

Deception is one of the quickest ways to gain little things and lose big things.